# interchange

English for international communication
## Jack C. Richards

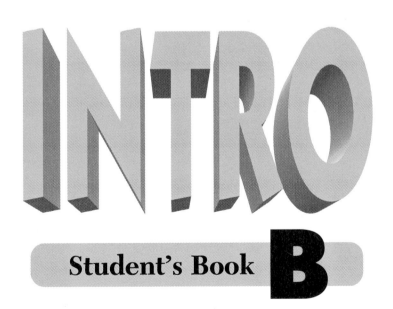

# INTRO

## Student's Book B

CAMBRIDGE
UNIVERSITY PRESS

Published by the Press Syndicate of the University of Cambridge
The Pitt Building, Trumpington Street, Cambridge CB2 1RP
40 West 20th Street, New York, NY 10011-4211, USA
10 Stamford Road, Oakleigh, Melbourne, Australia

First published 1994
Second Printing 1995

Printed in the United States of America

*Library of Congress Cataloging-in-Publication Data*
Richards, Jack C.
Interchange : English for international communication : intro
student's book / Jack C. Richards.
p. cm.
ISBN 0-521-46744-6
1. English language - Textbooks for foreign speakers.
2. Communication. International - Problems, exercises, etc.
I. Title. II. Title: Intro student's book.
PE1128.R456   1994                              94-17933
428.2´4 - dc20                                  CIP


ISBN 0 521 46744 6     Intro Student's Book
ISBN 0 521 46742 X     Intro Teacher's Manual
ISBN 0 521 46743 8     Intro Workbook
ISBN 0 521 46741 1     Intro Class Cassettes

*Split editions:*
ISBN 0 521 47185 0     Intro Student's Book A
ISBN 0 521 47186 9     Intro Student's Book B
ISBN 0 521 47187 7     Intro Workbook A
ISBN 0 521 47188 5     Intro Workbook B
ISBN 0 521 46740 3     Intro Student Cassette A
ISBN 0 521 47189 3     Intro Student Cassette B

Book design: Peter Ducker
Layout and design services: Adventure House, McNally Graphic Design
Cover design: Tom Wharton

Illustrators:
Randy Jones
Mark Kaufman
Beth McNally
Wally Neibart
Eva Sakmar-Sullivan
Bill Thomson
Sam Viviano

# Contents

# Plan of Intro Book B

|  | Topics | Functions | Grammar |
|---|---|---|---|
| **UNIT 9** | **Topics** Basic foods, desserts, and meals | **Functions** Naming foods; talking about food likes and dislikes; talking about eating habits | **Grammar** Countable and uncountable nouns; *some* and *any;* frequency adverbs *always, usually, often, sometimes, seldom, never* |
| **UNIT 10** | **Topics** Games, sports, and talents | **Functions** Asking for and giving information about abilities and talents | **Grammar** *Can* for ability: affirmative and negative statements, yes/no questions and short answers; *be good at* and *know how to* |
| **UNIT 11** | **Topics** Dates, birthdays, and celebrations | **Functions** Saying dates; asking about birthdays; asking about future plans | **Grammar** Ordinal numbers 1–100, future with *going to;* future time expressions; adjectives with *too*<br><br>**Listening** Listening to people |
| **UNIT 12** | **Topics** The body, health, problems, and advice | **Functions** Talking about illnesses and health problems; making appointments; giving advice | **Grammar** Time expressions: *in, on,* and *at;* affirmative and negative imperatives |

## Review of Units 9–12

|  | Topics | Functions | Grammar |
|---|---|---|---|
| **UNIT 13** | **Topics** Stores, locations in a city, and tourist attractions | **Functions** Giving information about shopping; asking for and giving locations and directions | **Grammar** Prepositions of place; more imperatives; adverbs *right* and *left* |
| **UNIT 14** | **Topics** Weekend activities | **Functions** Asking for and giving information about activities in the recent past | **Grammar** Past tense of regular and irregular verbs: affirmative and negative statements; yes/no questions and short answers |
| **UNIT 15** | **Topics** Biographical information and the lives of famous people | **Functions** Asking for and giving information about date and place of birth; talking about famous people | **Grammar** Past tense of *be:* affirmative and negative statements, yes/no questions and short answers; Wh-questions with *did, was,* and *were* |
| **UNIT 16** | **Topics** Home telecommunications and invitations | **Functions** Making phone calls; leaving messages on answering machines; inviting people and accepting and declining invitations | **Grammar** Prepositions of place *in, on,* and *at;* subject and object pronouns; verb + *to* + verb |

## Review of Units 13–16

## Interchange Activities

# Introduction

*Interchange* is a multi-level course in English as a second or foreign language for young adults and adults. The course covers the skills of listening, speaking, reading, and writing, with particular emphasis on listening and speaking. The primary goal of the course is to teach communicative competence – that is, the ability to communicate in English according to the situation, purpose, and roles of the participants. *Interchange* reflects the fact that English is the world's major language of international communication and is not limited to any one country, region, or culture. The *Intro* level is designed for beginning students needing a thorough presentation of basic functions, grammar, and vocabulary. It prepares students to enter Level 1 of the course.

## COURSE LENGTH

*Interchange* is a self-contained course covering all four language skills. Each level covers between 60 and 90 hours of class instruction time. Depending on how the book is used, however, more or less time may be utilized. The Teacher's Manual gives detailed suggestions for optional activities to extend each unit. Where less time is available, a level can be taught in approximately 60 hours by reducing the amount of time spent on Interchange Activities, reading, writing, optional activities, and the Workbook.

## COURSE COMPONENTS OF INTRO

**Student's Book** The Student's Book contains sixteen units, with a review unit after every four units. There are four review units in all. Following Unit 16 is a set of communicative activities called Interchange Activities, one for each unit of the book. Word lists at the end of the Student's Book contain key vocabulary and expressions used in each unit. The Student's Book is available in split edition, A and B, each containing 8 units.

**Teacher's Manual** A separate Teacher's Manual contains detailed suggestions on how to teach the course, lesson-by-lesson notes, an extensive set of follow-up activities, complete answer keys to the Student's Book and Workbook exercises, four tests for use in class, test answer keys, and transcripts of those listening activities not printed in the Student's Book or in the tests. The tests can be photocopied

and distributed to students after each review unit is completed.

**Workbook** The Workbook contains stimulating and varied exercises that provide additional practice on the teaching points presented in the Student's Book. A variety of exercise types is used to develop students' skills in grammar, reading, writing, spelling, vocabulary, and pronunciation. The Workbook can be used both for classwork and for homework. The Workbook is available in split editions.

**Class Cassettes** A set of cassettes for class use accompanies the Student's Book. The cassettes contain recordings of the word power activities, conversations, grammar focus summaries, pronunciation exercises, listening activities, and readings, as well as recordings of the listening exercises used in the tests. A variety of native-speaker voices and accents is used, along with some non-native speakers of English. Exercises that are recorded on the cassettes are indicated with the symbol ▭.

**Student Cassettes** Two cassettes are available for students to use for self-study. The Student Cassettes contain selected recordings of conversations, grammar, and pronunciation exercises from the Student's Book. Student Cassette A corresponds to Units 1–8 and Student Cassette B to Units 9–16.

## APPROACH AND METHODOLOGY

*Interchange* teaches students to use English for everyday situations and purposes related to work, school, social life, and leisure. The underlying philosophy of the course is that learning a second language is more rewarding, meaningful, and effective when the language is used for authentic communication. Information-sharing activities provide a maximum amount of student-generated communication. Throughout *Interchange,* students have the opportunity to personalize the language they learn and make use of their own life experiences and world knowledge.

The course has the following key features:

**Integrated Syllabus** *Interchange* has an integrated, multi-skills syllabus that links grammar and communicative functions. The course recognizes grammar as an essential component of second language proficiency. However, it presents grammar communicatively, with controlled accuracy-based activities leading to fluency-based communicative practice. The syllabus also contains the four skills of listening, speaking, reading, and writing, as well as pronunciation and vocabulary.

**Adult and International Content**   *Interchange* deals with contemporary topics that are of high interest and relevance to both students and teachers. Each unit includes real-world information on a variety of topics.

**Enjoyable and Useful Learning Activities** A wide variety of interesting and enjoyable activities forms the basis for each unit. The course makes extensive use of pair work, small group activities, role plays, and information-sharing activities. Practice exercises allow for a maximum amount of individual student practice and enable learners to personalize and apply the language they learn. Throughout the course, natural and useful language is presented that can be used in real-life situations.

# WHAT EACH UNIT OF INTRO CONTAINS

Each unit in *Interchange* contains the following kinds of exercises:

**Snapshot**   The Snapshots provide interesting information about the world, introduce the topic of the unit and develop vocabulary. The teacher can either present these exercises in class as reading or discussion activities, or have students read them by themselves in class or for homework, using their dictionaries if necessary.

**Conversation**   The Conversations introduce the new grammar of each unit in a communicative context and present functions and conversational expressions. The teacher can either present the Conversations with the Class Cassettes or read the dialogs aloud.

**Pronunciation**   These exercises focus on important features of spoken English, including stress, rhythm, intonation, reductions, and sound contrasts.

**Grammar Focus**   The new grammar of each unit is presented in color panels and is followed by practice activities that move from controlled to freer practice. These activities always give students a chance to use the grammar they have learned for real communication.

**Listening**   The listening activities develop a wide variety of listening skills, including listening for gist, listening for details, and inferring meaning from context. These exercises often require completing an authentic task while listening, such as taking telephone messages. The recordings offer natural conversational English with the pauses, hesitations, and interruptions that occur in real speech.

**Word Power**   The Word Power activities develop students' vocabulary through a variety of interesting tasks, such as word maps. Most of these are recorded.

**Writing**   The writing exercises include practical writing tasks that extend and reinforce the teaching points in the unit and introduce students to composition skills. The Teacher's Manual shows how to use these exercises to focus on the process of writing.

**Reading**   Beginning in Unit 5, there are reading passages designed to develop a variety of reading skills, including guessing words from context, skimming, scanning, and making inferences. Various text types adapted from authentic sources are included.

**Interchange Activities**   The Interchange Activities are pair work and group work tasks involving information sharing and role playing to encourage real communication. These exercises are a central part of the course and allow students to extend and personalize what they have learned in each unit.

# 9 I love strawberries!

## 1 WORD POWER 🔲

Match the foods to the words in the chart. Then listen and practice.
Add two more foods to each category.

*These are bananas . . .*

**BASIC FOODS**

| Fruit | Vegetables | Starches | Dairy | Meat and fish |
|---|---|---|---|---|
| ....... apples | ....... broccoli | ....... beans | ....... butter | ....... beef |
| ..*a*.. bananas | ....... carrots | ....... bread | ....... cheese | ....... chicken |
| ....... mangoes | ....... green beans | ....... pasta | ....... eggs | ....... lamb |
| ....... oranges | ....... peppers | ....... potatoes | ....... milk | ....... salmon |
| ....... strawberries | ....... tomatoes | ....... rice | ....... yogurt | ....... shrimp |
| ......................... | ......................... | ......................... | ......................... | ......................... |
| ......................... | ......................... | ......................... | ......................... | ......................... |

# 2 | **GRAMMAR FOCUS:** Countable vs. uncountable 📼

| Countable | | | Uncountable | |
|---|---|---|---|---|
| **singular** | **plural** | | **singular only** | |
| an apple | apples | I'm eating **an apple.** | yogurt | I'm eating **yogurt.** |
| a carrot | carrots | **Apples** are my favorite fruit. | beef | **Yogurt** is delicious. |
| a potato | potatoes | I like **apples.** | broccoli | I love **yogurt.** |

**1**   Divide the words in the chart on page 56 into two lists.

| *countable* | | *uncountable* | |
|---|---|---|---|
| apples | | broccoli | |
| | | | |
| | | | |

**2**   *Pair work*   Cover the chart on page 56 and identify the foods.

A: I think these are carrots.
B: Right. And this is broccoli.

**3**   Complete these sentences with **is** or **are**. Listen to check your answers.

a) Strawberries .................... my favorite fruit. I love strawberries!
b) I think mangoes ...................... delicious.
c) Green beans .................... my favorite vegetable.
d) Broccoli .................. very good for you.
e) I think cheese .................. awful. I hate cheese!
f) Chicken ...................... my favorite meat.

**4**   *Pair work*   Write responses to the items below.
Then compare information with a partner.

a) Name two foods you hate.
b) Name two foods you love.
c) Name three foods that are good for you.
d) What's your favorite fruit?
e) What's your favorite vegetable?
f) What's your favorite meat?

I hate broccoli . . .
Mangoes are my favorite fruit . . .

*fruit and vegetable market*

A: I hate broccoli. Do you like broccoli?
B: Yes, I do. But I hate peppers. Do you like peppers?
A: No, I don't . . .

# 3 PRONUNCIATION: Word stress 📼

Listen and notice the stress in these words. Find one more example of each pattern.

| *stress on first syllable* | *stress on second syllable* |
| --- | --- |
| **ap**ple | po**ta**toes |
| **straw**berries | to**ma**toes |
| ................................... | ................................... |

# 4 CONVERSATION 📼

Listen and practice.

Charles: What do we need for the barbecue?
Anne: Well, we need hamburger meat and hot dogs.
Charles: We have some hamburger in the freezer, but we don't have any hot dogs.
Anne: Right, and there aren't any buns.
Charles: Do we need any soda?
Anne: Yes, we do. Let's buy some soda and some lemonade, too.
Charles: All right. And how about some potato salad?
Anne: Great idea! Everyone likes potato salad.

# 5 LISTENING 📼

Listen to the rest of the conversation. Which desserts do Charles and Anne choose? Complete their shopping list.

cake    pie    cookies    ice cream    chocolate

| SHOPPING LIST |
| --- |
| hot dogs |
| buns |
| drinks |
| – – soda |
| – – lemonade |
| potato salad |
| dessert |
| – – |
| – – |

# 6 GRAMMAR FOCUS: *some, any* 🔲

| Affirmative statements | Questions and negative statements | |
|---|---|---|
| We need **some vegetables**. | Do you want **any carrots**? | We don't need **any carrots**. |
| We need **some meat**. | Do you want **any chicken**? | We don't need **any chicken**. |
| We need **some**. | Do you want **any**? | We don't need **any**. |

**1** Complete the conversation with **some** or **any**. Then practice with a partner.

Charles: Let's not buy potato salad. Let's make .................. .
Anne: OK. So we need .................. potatoes and .................. mayonnaise.
Charles: Is there .................. mayonnaise at home?
Anne: No, we need to buy .................. .
Charles: OK. Oh, we need .................. onions, too.
Anne: I don't want .................. onions in the salad. I hate onions!
Charles: Then let's buy .................. celery. That's good in potato salad.
Anne: Good idea. And .................. carrots, too.
Charles: Sure. There are .................. over there.

**2** *Pair work* What do you need from the supermarket today? Make a list. Then compare with a partner.

A: I need some bread.
B: I don't need any bread, but I need some rice.

# 7 SNAPSHOT

## TRADITIONAL BREAKFASTS

**U.S.A.**

orange juice, eggs, bacon or sausage, toast, and coffee

**Japan**

soup, fish, rice, pickles, and green tea

**Mexico**

eggs, tortillas, beans, hot peppers, fresh fruit, and coffee

What is a traditional breakfast in your country? ..................................................
What is your favorite meal? ..................................................

# 8 CONVERSATION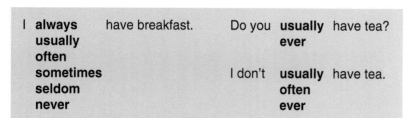

Listen and practice.

Sarah: Let's have breakfast together on Sunday.
Kumiko: OK. But why don't you come to my house? On Sundays my family has a Japanese-style breakfast.
Sarah: Really? What do you have?
Kumiko: We usually have fish, rice, and soup.
Sarah: Fish? Now that's interesting.
Kumiko: We sometimes have salad, too. And we always have green tea.
Sarah: Well, I don't often eat fish for breakfast, but I love to try new things.

# 9 GRAMMAR FOCUS: Frequency adverbs

| I | **always** | have breakfast. | Do you | **usually** | have tea? |
| | **usually** | | | **ever** | |
| | **often** | | | | |
| | **sometimes** | | I don't | **usually** | have tea. |
| | **seldom** | | | **often** | |
| | **never** | | | **ever** | |

| | |
|---|---|
| 100 % | **always** |
| | **usually** |
| | **often** |
| | **sometimes** |
| | **seldom** |
| 0 % | **never** |

**1** *Pair work* Add the adverbs to the sentences. Then practice the conversation with a partner.

A: What do you have for breakfast? (usually)
B: Well, I have eggs, bacon, and toast on Sundays. (often)
A: Do you eat breakfast at work? (ever)
B: Yes, I have breakfast at my desk. (sometimes)
A: Do you eat rice for breakfast? (ever)
B: I don't have rice. (often)

**2** *Pair work* Add three questions of your own. Then ask and answer questions with a partner.

a) Do you usually have breakfast in the morning?
b) What do you usually eat?
c) Do you ever eat meat or fish for breakfast?
d) Do you ever go to a restaurant for breakfast?
e) Do you always drink the same thing for breakfast?
f) Name one thing you never have for breakfast.

# 10 READING 🔊

**1**  Match the letters in the picture to the paragraphs.

## The Hamburger

You probably think that the hamburger is a typical American food. Americans often have a hamburger for a quick lunch or snack. But do you know that the favorite American "fast food" actually comes from many different countries?

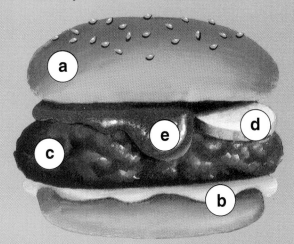

........ The **hamburger** is made of beef, not ham. The idea of chopping meat into very small pieces comes from Turkey. The name *hamburger* comes from the town of Hamburg in Germany.

........ The **pickle**, or pickled cucumber, comes from Eastern Europe. It is popular in Poland and Russia.

........ The word **ketchup** comes from China. "Ke-tsiap" is the Chinese name for a sauce made of pickled fish and spices. The first recipe for tomato ketchup is in a 1792 American cookbook.

........ **Mayonnaise**, sometimes called "mayo," is a yellow-white sauce made of eggs, oil, and lemon juice. It comes from the Spanish island of Minorca, but its name is French. Mayonnaise is also used as a dressing for salads.

........ The **bun** is a kind of bread. It comes from an English recipe, and the sesame seeds on top come from the Middle East.

So, the "American" hamburger is a truly international meal!

**2**  Answer these questions.

a) What different countries does the hamburger come from? Make a chart.

| ingredients | country of origin |
| --- | --- |
| .................... | .................... |
| .................... | .................... |

b) What other things do people put on hamburgers? What do you like on a hamburger?

c) What do you need to make your favorite sandwich, snack, or dessert? Write about it.

> ▶ **Interchange 9: Planning a picnic**
> Turn to page IC-12 and plan a picnic with three other students.

*My favorite sandwich is . . . To make the sandwich, you need . . .*

# 10 Can you swim very well?

## 1 SNAPSHOT

**SOME OLYMPIC SPORTS**

And countries with the most gold medals in these sports since 1952

**Winter Games**

speed skating
Former Soviet Union: 24

downhill skiing
Austria: 8

**Summer Games**

free-style swimming
United States: 34

marathon
Ethiopia: 3

What is your favorite winter sport? ................................................
What is your favorite summer sport? ................................................
What is your favorite Olympic sport? ................................................

## 2 CONVERSATION 🔊

Listen and practice.

Katherine: It's really hot. Let's go to the pool.
Philip: OK, but I can't swim very well.
Katherine: Well, I can't, either. I can only swim ten laps.
Philip: Ten laps? I can't even swim across the pool!
Katherine: But I can't dive at all. Can you dive?
Philip: Well, yes, I can. In fact, I can dive quite well.
Katherine: So, let's go. I can teach you how to swim, and you can teach me how to dive.

# **3** GRAMMAR FOCUS: *can* with abilities 🔊

| | | | you | | | | I | |
|---|---|---|---|---|---|---|---|---|
| You | | | I | | | | you | |
| She | **can** | swim. | **Can** | she | **swim** very well? | Yes, | she | **can.** |
| He | **can't** | | | he | | No, | he | **can't.** |
| We | | | we | | | | we | |
| They | | | they | | | | they | |

**1**   Katherine is talking about what she **can** and **can't** do.
Listen and practice.

a) I ............. draw.

b) I ............. write poetry.

c) I ............. fix a car.

d) I ............. play the piano.

e) I ............. sing very well.

f) I ............. cook very well.

**2**   *Pair work*   Complete the sentences above with
your own information. Compare with a partner.
Use **too** or **either**.

A:  I can cook.
B:  I can cook, too. I can't draw.
A:  I can't draw, either. But I can sing very well.
B:  I can't sing.

**3** *Group work*   Make a circle. Find out what special talents your classmates have. Ask about these abilities.

Juan:     Keiko, can you dance?
Keiko:    Yes, I can. Tai-lin, can you dance?
Tai-lin:  No, I can't. Can you dance, Ana? . . .

---

## 4 | PRONUNCIATION: *can* and *can't* 🔲

**1**   Listen and practice. Notice that **can** is reduced.

/kən/                    /kænt/
I **can** play the piano, but I **can't** sing very well.

**2**   *Pair work*   Read a sentence from list A or B. Your partner says "A" or "B."

| A | B |
|---|---|
| I can dance. | I can't dance. |
| He can draw. | He can't draw. |
| She can sing. | She can't sing. |
| They can skate very well. | They can't skate very well. |

---

## 5 | CONVERSATION 🔲

Listen and practice.

Matthew: What's your new girlfriend like?
Philip:    Katherine? Well, she's good at languages.
Matthew: Does she know how to speak Spanish?
Philip:    She knows how to speak Spanish *and* Japanese.
Matthew: Wow!
Philip:    And she's good at sports, too. She knows how to play tennis and basketball.
Matthew: That's terrific.
Philip:    But there's one thing she's not good at.
Matthew: What's that?
Philip:    She's not good at remembering things. We have a date, and she's an hour late!

# 6 WORD POWER: Sports 🔲

**1** Listen and practice.

*They're playing basketball.*

soccer

baseball

football

basketball

volleyball

golf

tennis

Ping-Pong

**2** Now complete the chart. Add two more sports to each category.

| team sports | individual sports |
|---|---|
| basketball | |
| | |
| | |
| | |
| | |

**3** *Pair work* Ask a partner about sports abilities.

A: Do you know how to play basketball?
B: Yes, I do. (No, I don't.)

## 7 GRAMMAR FOCUS: *be good at; know how to* 🔲

Is your girlfriend **good at** sports?
She**'s good at** team sports.

She **knows how to play** basketball,
but she **doesn't know how to play** baseball.

**1** *Pair work*   Add five more questions.
Then interview a partner.

a) Are you good at languages?
b) Do you know how to speak Japanese, Spanish, or Russian?
c) What languages can you speak fluently?
d) Are you good at sports?
e) Do you know how to play soccer?
f) Are you good at winter sports?
g) Do you know how to ski or ice-skate?
h) Are you good at card games?
i) What card games do you know how to play?
j) Are you good at board games?
k) Do you know how to play chess?
l) What board games do you know how to play?
m) Are you good at video games?
n) ................................................ ?
o) ................................................ ?
p) ................................................ ?
q) ................................................ ?
r) ................................................ ?

**2**   Write five sentences about your partner.
Read them to the class.

*Keiko is good at languages. She can speak Spanish fluently. She isn't good at sports, but . . .*

*a board game: Scrabble*

*chess*

*a card game*

*a video game*

## 8 LISTENING 🔲

Listen to questions and choose the best response.

a) ☐ No, I can't.          c) ☐ Yes, I can.          e) ☐ No, I don't.
   ☐ No, I don't.             ☐ Yes, I do.                ☐ No, I can't.

b) ☐ Yes, I can.          d) ☐ Yes, I can.          f) ☐ No, I don't.
   ☐ Yes, I do.              ☐ Yes, I do.                ☐ No, I can't.

# 9 READING 📼

## Amazing animals

Do you know that the kangaroo can't walk at all – but it can travel at 40 miles an hour! This amazing animal is very good at jumping. It can jump 20 feet at a time. An adult kangaroo is only five feet tall, but it can jump over a car.

The camel can live without water for one week. It can walk over 200 miles in the desert without drinking water. It can do this because it has three stomachs that hold water. And the hump on its back holds fat, so the camel can live without food for a long time, too.

The chimpanzee is a very intelligent animal that is good at learning language. A chimpanzee can learn to use sign language, but it can't always use correct grammar. For example, a chimpanzee can use sign language to say, "Me want banana now," but not, "I want a banana now, please."

**1**  Read about these animals and then fill in the chart.

|  | *Can* | *Can't* |
|---|---|---|
| Kangaroo | ............................................. | ............................................. |
| Camel | ............................................. | ............................................. |
| Chimpanzee | ............................................. | ............................................. |

**2**  Do you know something interesting about an animal? Write about it.

*A giraffe can clean its eyes and ears with its tongue . . .*

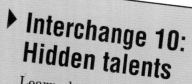

▶ **Interchange 10: Hidden talents**

Learn about your classmates' special abilities. Turn to page IC-13.

# 11 When's your birthday?

1 ## SNAPSHOT

**INGREDIENTS FOR A HAPPY BIRTHDAY**

**Popular birthday months**

More people are born in August than any other month. September is the second most popular month.

Fewest people are born in April and May.

"Happy Birthday to You"

birthday party

birthday presents

birthday card    birthday cake with candles

Do you celebrate your birthday every year? ...............................................................................
What do you usually do? ...............................................................................

## 2 DATES 🔲

**1** Listen and practice the months.

| | |
|---|---|
| January | July |
| February | August |
| March | September |
| April | October |
| May | November |
| June | December |

**AUGUST**

| SUN | MON | TUE | WED | THU | FRI | SAT |
|---|---|---|---|---|---|---|
| 1 | 2 | 3 | 4 | 5 | 6 | 7 |
| 8 | 9 | 10 | 11 | 12 | 13 | 14 |
| 15 | 16 | 17 | 18 | 19 | 20 | 21 |
| 22 | 23 | 24 | 25 | 26 | 27 | 28 |
| 29 | 30 | 31 | | | | |

**2** Listen and practice the numbers.

| | | | | | | | |
|---|---|---|---|---|---|---|---|
| 1st | first | 11th | eleventh | 21st | twenty-first | 31st | thirty-first |
| 2nd | second | 12th | twelfth | 22nd | twenty-second | . . . | |
| 3rd | third | 13th | thirteenth | 23rd | twenty-third | 40th | fortieth |
| 4th | fourth | 14th | fourteenth | 24th | twenty-fourth | 50th | fiftieth |
| 5th | fifth | 15th | fifteenth | 25th | twenty-fifth | 60th | sixtieth |
| 6th | sixth | 16th | sixteenth | 26th | twenty-sixth | 70th | seventieth |
| 7th | seventh | 17th | seventeenth | 27th | twenty-seventh | 80th | eightieth |
| 8th | eighth | 18th | eighteenth | 28th | twenty-eighth | 90th | ninetieth |
| 9th | ninth | 19th | nineteenth | 29th | twenty-ninth | 100th | hundredth |
| 10th | tenth | 20th | twentieth | 30th | thirtieth | | |

**3** Now practice these dates.

a) January 1st (January first)
b) May 23rd (May twenty-third)
c) 6/31 (June thirty-first)

d) July 4th
e) August 29th
f) September 30th

g) 2/1
h) 4/21
i) 10/4

# 3 CLASS SURVEY

**1** Find out your classmates' birthdays. Make a list.

A: When is your birthday?
B: July 28th. When is your birthday?

| Name | Birthday |
|------|----------|
| Juan | June 21st |
| Keiko | January 3rd |

**2** *Class activity*   Compare information with your classmates.

How many people have birthdays . . .
   this week? ............
   this month? ............
   in the same month? ............
   on the same day? ............

# 4 CONVERSATION 🔲

**1** Listen and practice.

Amy:    How old are you, Philip?
Philip:  I'm twenty years old. But I'm going to be twenty-one on August 5th.
Amy:    That's next Friday! What are you going to do?
Philip:  Katherine is going to take me to a restaurant.
Amy:    Nice! Is she going to order a birthday cake?
Philip:  Probably. And the waiters are probably going to sing "Happy Birthday" to me. It's so embarrassing.
Amy:    Oh, I bet it's going to be fun.
Philip:  I don't know. I hope so.

**2** Listen to the rest of the conversation and answer the questions.

a) When is Amy's birthday? How old is she going to be?
b) What is she going to do on her birthday?

# **5** **GRAMMAR FOCUS:** Future with *going to*

| I'm<br>You're<br>He's     **(not) going to work** tonight.<br>She's<br>We're<br>They're | Are you **going to work** late?<br>    Yes, I am. (No, I'm not.)<br><br>What are you **going to do** after work?<br>    I'm **going to have** dinner. | **Time expressions**<br><br>tonight<br>tomorrow<br>tomorrow night<br>next week<br>next Saturday<br>next month |
| --- | --- | --- |

**1**   Are you going to do any of these things tonight? Write ten sentences. Compare with a partner.

| *Things I'm going to do tonight* | *Things I'm not going to do tonight* |
| --- | --- |
| I'm going to see a movie. | I'm not going to clean the house. |
| | |
| | |
| | |
| | |

**2**  *Pair work*   Ask about your partner's plans for tonight.

A: Are you going to go to a movie tonight?
B: Yes, I am. (No, I'm not.)

**3**  *Pair work*   Now ask and answer questions about your plans for the times in the box.

A: What are you going to do tomorrow night?
B: I'm going to stay home and watch television.
   What about you? What are you going to do? . . .

| tomorrow night<br>next Saturday night<br>next Sunday<br>next summer<br>on your next birthday |
| --- |

# 6 PRONUNCIATION: *going to* 📼

**1**  Listen to how **going to** is pronounced.

A: What are you **going to** do tonight?
B: I'm **going to** stay home.

> **Going to** is pronounced /ɡənə/ in conversation.

**2**  Now listen and practice.

A: What are you **going to** do for your birthday?
B: I'm **going to** go out with some friends.
A: Where are you **going to** go?
B: We're **going to** go to a restaurant.

# 7 LISTENING 📼

**1**  It's five thirty in the evening and these people are waiting for the bus.
What do you think they are going to do tonight? Write one guess for each person.

|  | *My guess* | *What they are going to do* |
|---|---|---|
| Michelle | ................................................ | ................................................ |
| Kevin | ................................................ | ................................................ |
| Robert | ................................................ | ................................................ |
| Jane | ................................................ | ................................................ |

**2**  Now listen to the people tell about their evening plans.
What are they actually going to do?

# 8 CELEBRATIONS

*Pair work*   What are these people doing? What are they going to do? Write four sentences about each picture, using the expressions in the box below. Then compare sentences with a partner.

a) It's Jeremy's birthday . . .

b) It's New Year's Eve . . .

c) It's Jessica's high school graduation . . .

d) It's the Fourth of July in the U.S. . . .

| | |
|---|---|
| blow out the candles | receive some presents |
| sing "Happy Birthday" | have a party |
| open the presents | wear special hats |
| shout "Happy New Year" | have a good time |
| kiss their friends | have a picnic |
| listen to a speech | cook food on the barbecue |
| receive a diploma | watch the fireworks |

▶ **Interchange 11: Vacation plans**

Talk about your next vacation or a "dream" vacation. Turn to page IC-14.

# 9 READING 📼

## What are you going to do on your birthday?

**Elena Buenaventura, Madrid, Spain:**
"My twenty-first birthday is on Saturday, and I'm going to go out with some friends. To wish me a happy birthday, they're going to pull on my ear 21 times, once for each year. It's an old custom. Some people do it only once, but my friends are very traditional!"

**Mr. and Mrs. Isai, Kyoto, Japan:**
"My husband is going to be 60 tomorrow. In Japan, the sixtieth birthday is called *kanreki* – it's the beginning of a new life. The color red represents a new life, so we always give something red for a sixtieth birthday. What am I going to give my husband? I can't say. It's a surprise."

**Sun Hee Shi, Taipei, Taiwan:**
"Tomorrow is my sixteenth birthday. It's a special birthday, so we're going to have a family ceremony. I'm probably going to receive some money in 'lucky' envelopes from my relatives. My mother is going to cook noodles – noodles are for a long life."

**Philippe Joly, Paris, France:** "I'm going to be 30 next week. So I'm going to invite three very good friends out to dinner. In France, when you have a birthday, you often invite people out. I know that in some countries it's the opposite – people take you out."

**1** Read the four paragraphs. Then correct these statements.

a) To celebrate her birthday, Elena is going to pull on her friends' ears.
b) Sun Hee is going to cook some noodles on her birthday.
c) On his birthday, Mr. Isai is going to buy something red.
d) Philippe's friends are going to take him out to dinner on his birthday.

**2** Do you have plans for your next birthday, or for the birthday of a friend or family member? What are you going to do? Write several sentences.

*I'm going to be twenty-five on March 15th. I'm going to . . .*

# 12 What's the matter?

## 1 SNAPSHOT

**COMMON REASONS FOR MISSING CLASS**

a cold     a stomachache     the flu     feeling sad or "blue"     a "bad hair day"

What are other reasons to miss class? .............................................................................
Do you ever miss work or class? Why? .............................................................................

## 2 CONVERSATION 📼

Listen and practice.

Brian: Hi, Victor. How are you?
Victor: Oh, I'm fine.
Brian: So, are you going to go to class tonight?
Victor: Maybe, but I don't think so.
Brian: Really? What's the matter?
Victor: I don't know. I'm just feeling a little sad.
Brian: Listen. Come with me to class, and after class we can go out for dinner.
Victor: Now that's a good idea. Thanks a lot, Brian. I'm feeling better already.

# 3 HEALTH PROBLEMS 🔲

**1**   Listen. Point to each body part.

*Point to your head.*

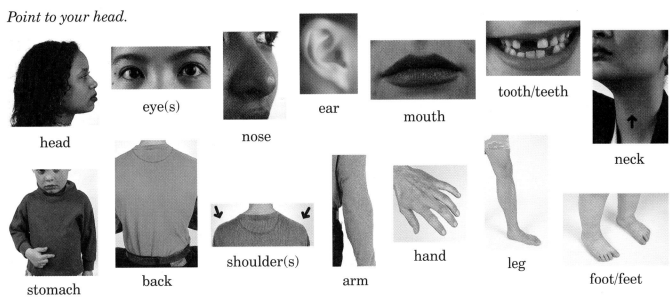

eye(s)

ear

mouth

tooth/teeth

head

nose

neck

shoulder(s)

hand

leg

stomach

back

arm

foot/feet

**2**   Listen and practice these conversations.

A: What's the matter?
B: I have a headache.
A: Oh, that's too bad.

A: What's wrong?
B: I have a sore throat.
A: Oh, I'm sorry to hear that.

A: How do you feel?
B: I feel terrible. I have a cold.
A: Well, I hope you feel better soon.

**3**   *Class activity*   Take turns acting out the illnesses below or other
health problems. Classmates guess what is wrong and give you sympathy.

A: Do you have a headache?
B: No, I don't.
C: Do you have an earache?
B: Yes, I do.
C: That's too bad!

| | | |
|---|---|---|
| a headache | the flu | a sore foot |
| a backache | a cold | a sore arm |
| a stomachache | a fever | a sore throat |
| an earache | | |

---

# 4 LISTENING 🔲

Listen to people talk about health problems. What's wrong with them?
Write the name of the body part where they have a problem.

a) ...............................................

b) ...............................................

c) ...............................................

d) ...............................................

e) ...............................................

f) ...............................................

## 5 PRONUNCIATION: Sentence stress 🔲

**1** Listen to the stressed syllables in each sentence. Then practice the sentences.

What's the **mat**ter?
I have a terrible **head**ache.
I have a very sore **throat**.

**2** *Class activity* Listen and underline the syllable with the strongest stress in each sentence. Then practice the conversation.

A: What's the problem?
B: I have a very high fever.
A: Are you taking some aspirin?
B: Yes, I am. And I'm drinking a lot of water.

## 6 CONVERSATION 🔲

Listen and practice.

Receptionist: Dr. Ryan's office.
Susan: Hello, this is Susan West. Can I make an appointment on Friday the 17th?
Receptionist: OK, Ms. West. In the morning or afternoon?
Susan: In the afternoon.
Receptionist: Can you come at 4:00 P.M.?
Susan: That's fine.

Dr. Ryan: And what's the problem, Ms. West?
Susan: I have a terrible backache. I can't even sit down.
Dr. Ryan: OK. Take these pills every four hours. Stay in bed this week. And don't lift heavy things.
Susan: Thanks, Dr. Ryan.

# 7 TIME EXPRESSIONS: *on, at,* and *in*

| | | |
|---|---|---|
| **in** the morning | **on** Monday | **at** 10:00 A.M. |
| **in** the afternoon | **on** Monday morning | **at** two o'clock |
| **in** the evening | **on** Mondays | **at** noon |
| **in** June | **on** July 15th | **at** midnight |
| **in** December | **on** the 15th (of July) | **at** night |
| **in** the summer | **on** weekdays | |
| | **on** weekends | |

*Pair work*   Complete the conversations. Then practice with a partner.

A: Are you free ......... Sunday? There's a party at Victoria's place.
B: Is the party ......... the afternoon?
A: No, it starts ......... 8:00 P.M.
B: But I never go to parties ......... Sunday nights. I go to work ......... 7:30 A.M. Monday.
A: But the party is ......... July 3rd. You don't work ......... the Fourth of July. It's a holiday.

A: Can I make an appointment ......... June? I'm free ......... Wednesdays.
B: Can you come ......... Wednesday the 7th?
A: ......... the 7th, I can only come ......... the morning.
B: I have an opening ......... ten ......... the morning.
A: Good. So the appointment is ......... Wednesday the 7th ......... 10:00 A.M.
B: That's right. See you then.

A: Can I have an appointment ......... Tuesday the 6th?
B: ......... the morning?
A: No, ......... the afternoon, please.
B: Can you come ......... three o'clock?
A: That's fine. So my appointment is ......... three o'clock ......... the 13th.
B: Well, no, it's ......... Tuesday the 6th. By the way, what's your problem?
A: I have trouble remembering things. When is my appointment again?

# [8] GRAMMAR FOCUS: Imperatives 📼

| Affirmative | Negative |
| --- | --- |
| **Take** these pills. | **Don't drink** coffee. |
| **Stay** in bed. | **Don't lift** heavy things. |
| | **Don't forget** your doctor's appointment. |

**1** What are these people saying? Choose from the sentences in the box. Compare with a partner.

I have a headache.
I can't sleep at night.
My job is very stressful.
I have a fever.
I can't lose weight.
I have a stomachache.
There's no food in the house.

a

b

c

d

e

f

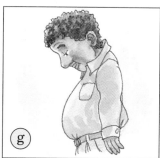
g

**2** *Pair work*   What is your advice for the people above?
Choose from the list below or think of your own advice.

A: I have a fever.
B: Take two aspirin . . .

Don't drink coffee or tea in the evening.

Don't eat desserts.

Go out to a restaurant.

Go to bed and sleep.

Go home and relax.

Eat some toast and drink some tea.

Don't go to work.

Take a hot bath at night.

Take two aspirin and drink a lot of water.

Don't eat any food for a day.

Get some exercise every day.

Go to a store and buy some food.

Go to bed early at night.

# 9 READING 🔊

## SECRETS OF A LONG LIFE

Sadie and Bessie Delany are sisters who live in Mount Vernon, New York. Sadie is 104 years old, and Bessie is 102. They tell their life story in a book called "Having Our Say: The Delany Sisters' First Hundred Years." Here is some of their advice for living a long, healthy life.

∗ Get up early. The Delany sisters get up at 6:30 or 7:00 A.M.

∗ Have a good breakfast. The sisters eat oatmeal, half a banana, bran, and eggs with a little cheese.

∗ Exercise every day. The Delany sisters like to do yoga. They also walk every day.

∗ Eat lots of vegetables, especially garlic. Garlic is good for your health, even if it's not good for your breath!

**BUT . . .**

∗ **Don't** eat a lot of salt and fat. These things are bad for you.

∗ **Don't** get married! The sisters say, "We are still alive because we don't have husbands who worry us."

∗ **Don't** listen to the doctor. "Most doctors don't know what to do with us," Sadie says. "When something's wrong they say, 'You're still living, what do you expect?'"

**1** Do you agree with Bessie and Sadie's advice? If you agree, write **yes**. If you don't agree, write some advice of your own.

Eat lots of vegetables. ......................................................

Don't get married. ......................................................

Exercise every day. ......................................................

Get up early. ......................................................

Don't eat a lot of salt or fat. ......................................................

Don't listen to the doctor. ......................................................

Eat a lot of garlic. ......................................................

Have a good breakfast. ......................................................

**2** Can you think of any more advice for living a long life? Write at least five sentences like these:

> *Drink a lot of juice. Don't eat desserts. Don't . . .*

▶**Interchange 12: Helpful advice**
Turn to page IC-15 and give advice for some common problems.

# Review of Units 9–12

## 1 Mealtime

*Pair work*   Complete the chart for each meal. Then ask and answer questions with a partner.

|  | *breakfast* | *lunch* | *dinner* |
|---|---|---|---|
| a) What time do you usually eat? | .................... | .................... | .................... |
| b) Where do you usually eat? | .................... | .................... | .................... |
| c) What do you usually have? | .................... | .................... | .................... |
|  | .................... | .................... | .................... |

## 2 Your favorite fruit

*Pair work*   Think of your favorite fruit. Your partner tries to guess it.

What color is it?
What color is it on the inside?
Can you eat the skin?
Does it have seeds or a pit?
Can you cook it?
What time of year can you buy it?

## 3 Listening: What's the matter? 🔲

Listen to these conversations. Match the conversation to the problem.

a) ..........   1) This person probably needs some ketchup.
b) ..........   2) This person probably has a backache.
c) ..........   3) This person probably can't dance very well.
d) ..........   4) This person is probably feeling sad.
e) ..........   5) This person is probably going to take a test tomorrow.
f) ..........   6) This person probably has the flu.

# 4 Abilities

*Pair work*   Write four sentences about your abilities. Your partner tries to guess what they are.

a) Name an artistic talent that you have.
   (Can you play a musical instrument, draw, dance, write poetry?)
b) Name a card or board game that you know how to play.
   (Do you know how to play chess? bridge?)
c) Name a sport that you are good at.
d) Name a food that you know how to cook.

A: Can you write poetry?
B: No, I can't.
A: Can you sing? . . .

# 5 Important dates

*Pair work*   Choose four important holidays or celebrations. What are the dates? What are you going to do? Tell your partner.

"Thanksgiving is on November 24th. I'm going to visit my parents. We're going to . . ."

# 6 Weekend plans

*Pair work*   Complete this datebook with your weekend plans. Then ask and answer questions with a partner.

A: What are you going to do on Friday evening?
B: I'm going to go to the movies.

| | Friday | Saturday | Sunday |
|---|---|---|---|
| 9:00 morning | | | |
| 10:00 | | | |
| 11:00 | | | |
| 12:00 | | | |
| 1:00 afternoon | | | |
| 2:00 | | | |
| 3:00 | | | |
| 4:00 | | | |
| 5:00 | | | |
| 6:00 evening | | | |
| 7:00 | | | |
| 8:00 | | | |
| 9:00 | | | |

# 7 Listening

Some people are getting ready for a barbecue. Listen to the questions. Choose the best response.

a) ☐ No, they have the flu.
   ☐ No, she isn't.

b) ☐ Yes, you can go.
   ☐ Yes, but we need some paper.

c) ☐ Yes, buy some.
   ☐ No, there aren't any.

d) ☐ No, I'm not.
   ☐ No, I don't.

e) ☐ No, we need some.
   ☐ No, we aren't.

f) ☐ No, I like chocolate cake.
   ☐ No, we don't have any.

# 13 Can you help me, please?

## 1 WORD POWER 📟

**1** Where can you buy these things? Match the items with the places. Then listen and practice.

*You can buy books at a bookstore.*

a) books ...5...

b) a fish dinner ..........

c) carrots ..........

d) stamps ..........

e) a television ..........

f) gasoline ..........

g) aspirin ..........

h) a magazine ..........

1) a supermarket

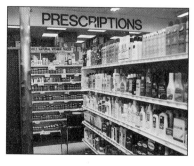
2) a drugstore

3) a newsstand

4) a restaurant

5) a bookstore

6) a department store

7) a gas station

8) a post office

82

**2** *Pair work*   Ask and answer these questions with a partner.

a) Where can you buy clothes?
b) Where can you have a hamburger?
c) Where can you buy furniture?
d) Name four places you can buy a magazine.
e) Who works at a department store? A restaurant?
f) Name three things you can buy at a newsstand.
g) Name three things you can buy at a drugstore.
h) Name five things you can buy at a supermarket.

# **2** PRONUNCIATION: Compound nouns 🔲

**1**   Listen and practice.

**post** office      **gas** station      **drug**store      **news**stand

**2**   Find four more expressions made of two words. Say them aloud.

.......................................      ...........................................

.......................................      ...........................................

# **3** CONVERSATION 🔲

Listen and practice.

Charles:  Can you help me, please? Is there a public
          restroom near here?
Woman:  I'm sorry, but I don't think so.
Charles:  Oh, no! My son needs a bathroom.
Woman:  Well, there's a department store on Grant
          Street. There are restrooms in the basement.
Charles:  Where on Grant Street?
Woman:  Between Second and Third Streets.
          The store is across from the hotel.
Charles:  Thank you very much.
Woman:  You're welcome.

# **4** LISTENING 🔲

What are these people going to buy? Where are they going to buy it?
Listen and complete the chart.

|  | *What* | *Where* |
|---|---|---|
| a) Sarah | .............................. | .............................. |
| b) Michael | .............................. | .............................. |
| c) Jennifer | .............................. | .............................. |
| d) Victor | .............................. | .............................. |

## **5** **GRAMMAR FOCUS:** Prepositions of place 📼

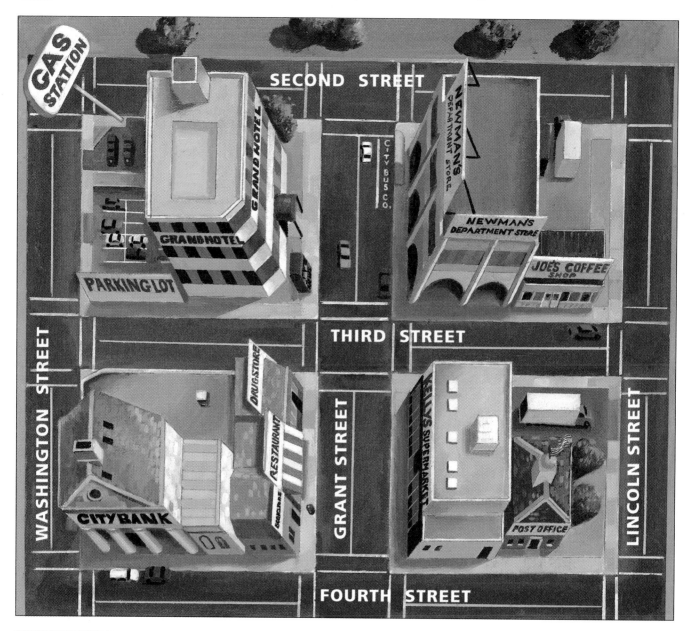

The department store is **on** Grant Street.
It's **between** Second and Third Streets.
It's **across from** the Grand Hotel.
There's a newsstand **in front of** the hotel.

There's a gas station **behind** the hotel.
The gas station is **on the corner of** Washington and Second.
The gas station is **next to** a parking lot.
The parking lot is **near** the City Bank.

**1** Look at the map and complete the sentences.

a) There's a bus stop .............. the department store.
b) There's a parking lot .............. the department store.
c) The parking lot is .............. the Grand Hotel.
d) There's a gas station .............. the parking lot.
e) There's a restaurant .............. Grant Street, .............. Third and Fourth Streets.
f) The restaurant is .............. a drugstore and a bookstore.
g) The bookstore is .............. Grant and Fourth.

**2** *Pair work* Look at the map on page 84 and complete the conversations. Then practice with a partner.

A: Excuse me, sir. Is there a restaurant .............. here?
B: Well, there's a new restaurant .............. Grant Street.
    It's .............. Kelly's Supermarket. But it's expensive.
A: Isn't there a coffee shop .............. Third Street?
B: Yes, it's .............. Lincoln and Third.

A: Excuse me, miss. Is there a gas station ..............
    Washington Street?
B: Yes, there is. It's .............. Washington and Second.
A: So it's .............. the Grand Hotel.
B: Right. And it's .............. a big parking lot.

**3** *Pair work* Ask and answer questions about your neighborhood.

A: Is there a bookstore near here?
B: Yes, there is. It's on Taylor Street, next to the post office.

---

# **6** LISTENING 🔲

Look at the map on page 84 as you listen to these conversations. Where are these people going?

a) ............................................
b) ............................................
c) ............................................

---

# **7** CONVERSATION 🔲

Listen and practice.

Tourist: Excuse me, ma'am. How do I get to
    St. Patrick's Cathedral?
Woman: Walk up Fifth Avenue to 50th Street.
    St. Patrick's is on the right.
Tourist: Is it near Rockefeller Center?
Woman: It's right across from Rockefeller Center.
Tourist: Thanks. And what about the Empire State Building?
    Is it far from here?
Woman: It's right behind you. Just turn around
    and look up!

# 8 SNAPSHOT

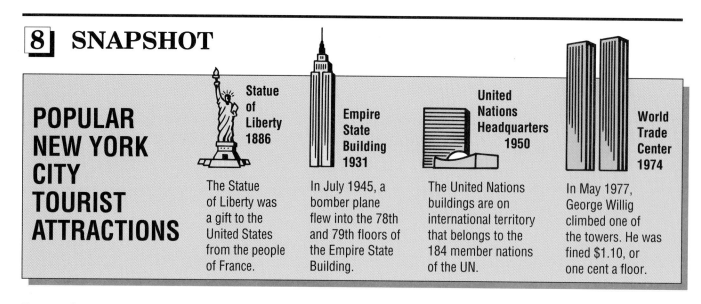

## POPULAR NEW YORK CITY TOURIST ATTRACTIONS

**Statue of Liberty 1886**

The Statue of Liberty was a gift to the United States from the people of France.

**Empire State Building 1931**

In July 1945, a bomber plane flew into the 78th and 79th floors of the Empire State Building.

**United Nations Headquarters 1950**

The United Nations buildings are on international territory that belongs to the 184 member nations of the UN.

**World Trade Center 1974**

In May 1977, George Willig climbed one of the towers. He was fined $1.10, or one cent a floor.

Do you know any other tourist attractions in New York City? ...................................................

What are some tourist attractions in your city? ...................................................

# 9 DIRECTIONS

Walk **down** Fifth Avenue **for ten blocks.**
     **up**                **to 50th Street.**

Turn **right** at 50th Street.
     **left**

The building is **on the right**.
                **on the left**.

Follow the directions as you look at the map. What building are you going to?

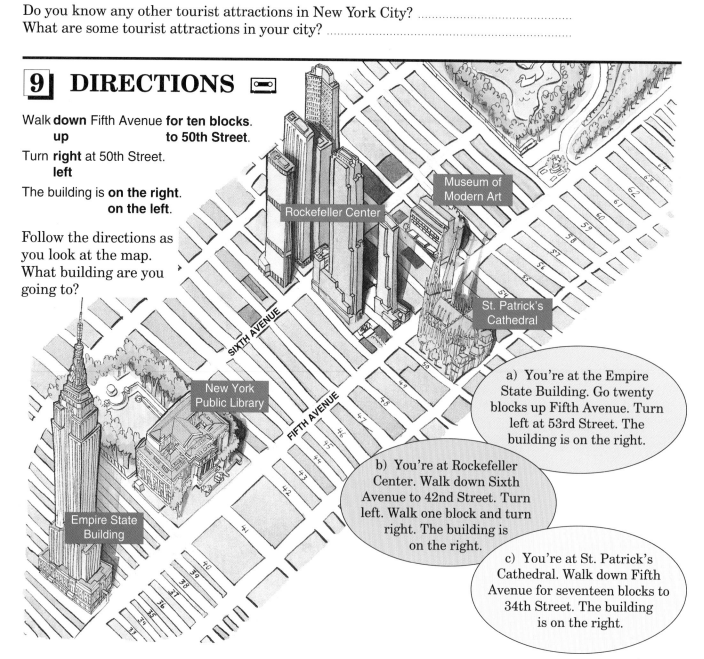

a) You're at the Empire State Building. Go twenty blocks up Fifth Avenue. Turn left at 53rd Street. The building is on the right.

b) You're at Rockefeller Center. Walk down Sixth Avenue to 42nd Street. Turn left. Walk one block and turn right. The building is on the right.

c) You're at St. Patrick's Cathedral. Walk down Fifth Avenue for seventeen blocks to 34th Street. The building is on the right.

# 10 READING 🔊

**1** As you read, follow the directions on the map on page 86.

## A walk up Fifth Avenue

Start your tour at the **Empire State Building,** on Fifth Avenue between 33rd and 34th Streets. This building has 102 floors. Take the elevator to the 102nd floor for a great **view** of New York City.

Walk up Sixth Avenue to 49th Street. You're standing in the middle of the 19 buildings of **Rockefeller Center**. Turn right on 49th Street, walk another block, and turn left. You're in Rockefeller Plaza. In the winter, there's a **rink** where you can ice-skate.

Now walk seven blocks up Fifth Avenue to the New York Public Library. The entrance is between 40th and 42nd Streets. This library holds over 10 million books. Behind the library is **Bryant Park**. In the summer, there's an outdoor café, and at lunch hour, there are free **music concerts**.

Right across from Rockefeller Center on Fifth Avenue is **St. Patrick's Cathedral**. It's modeled after the cathedral in Cologne, Germany. Go inside the cathedral and leave the noisy city behind. Look at the beautiful blue **windows**. Many of these windows come from France.

**2** Where can you do these things?

a) Where can you have a view of the city?
b) Where can you go skating in the winter?
c) Where can you listen to music outdoors?
d) Where can you sit quietly indoors?

**3** Write answers to the questions above.
Use information about your town.
Write two sentences for each question.

> In my town, you can listen to music in a park next to the river . . .

▶ **Interchange 13: Directions**

Give directions in a town. Student A turns to page IC-16 and Student B turns to page IC-18.

# 14 Did you have a good weekend?

## 1 SNAPSHOT

**THE WEEKEND IN THE U.S.A.**

Average free time on the weekend: 19 hours and 40 minutes.
How adults spend their free time:

watching television
5 hours and 19 minutes

talking to friends
1 hour and 40 minutes

reading
53 minutes

making or fixing things
43 minutes

shopping
43 minutes

taking a walk
34 minutes

doing other things
9 hours and 48 minutes

How much time do you spend on these activities? ....................................................................

## 2 WORD POWER

Add these activities to the word map.
Then add two activities to each category.

> fixing things     making things     reading
> shopping     taking a walk
> talking to friends     watching television

**WORK**
*cleaning the house*

**EXERCISE**
*swimming*

**WEEKEND ACTIVITIES**

**ENTERTAINMENT**
*going to a movie*

**RELAXATION**
*sleeping*

# 3 CONVERSATION

Listen and practice.

Michael: Hi, Nicole. Did you have a good weekend?
Nicole: Yes, I did. But I feel tired today.
Michael: Really? Why?
Nicole: Well, on Saturday I cleaned the house and played tennis. Then on Sunday I hiked in the country.
Michael: And I bet you studied, too.
Nicole: Yeah. I studied on Sunday evening. What about you?
Michael: Well, I didn't clean the house and I didn't study. I stayed in bed and watched TV.
Nicole: That sounds like fun, but did you exercise?
Michael: Sort of. I played golf on my computer.

# 4 GRAMMAR FOCUS: Past tense of regular verbs

| Regular verbs: verb + *ed* or *d* | | | Spelling |
|---|---|---|---|
| I | | | work**ed** |
| You | **studied** | | exercise**d** |
| She | **worked** | on Saturday. | stud**ied** |
| He | **exercised** | | play**ed** |
| We | | | |
| They | | | |

| | | |
|---|---|---|
| I | | |
| You | **didn't study** | |
| She | **didn't work** | on Sunday. |
| He | **didn't exercise** | |
| We | | |
| They | | |

**1** Read the conversation again. Then talk about Nicole's and Michael's weekends with a partner. Use these expressions:

| | |
|---|---|
| clean the house | hike in the country |
| study | play computer games |
| stay in bed | watch TV |
| exercise | play tennis |

A: Nicole cleaned the house.
B: Michael didn't clean the house.

**2** *Pair work* Write four things you did and four things you didn't do last weekend. Then compare with a partner. Use these or other expressions.

| wash my clothes | relax | invite friends to my house | rent a video |
| cook a meal | visit my family | work in the yard | listen to music |

| *Things I did last weekend* | *Things I didn't do last weekend* |
| --- | --- |
| I relaxed. | I didn't wash my clothes. |
| | |
| | |
| | |

A: I listened to music last weekend.
B: I didn't listen to music.
A: I didn't visit my family.
B: I didn't visit my family, either.

## 5 PRONUNCIATION: Past tense 📼

**1** Listen and practice. Notice the pronunciation of **d** and **ed**.

| /t/ | /d/ | /ɪd/ |
| --- | --- | --- |
| watch**ed** | play**ed** | invit**ed** |
| hik**ed** | clean**ed** | visit**ed** |
| .................... | .................... | .................... |
| .................... | .................... | .................... |
| .................... | .................... | .................... |
| .................... | .................... | .................... |

**2** Listen to these words. Add them to the lists above.

| started | missed | attended | asked | loved | washed |
| fixed | walked | opened | listened | skated | hated |

# 6 CONVERSATION

Listen and practice.

Laura: So did you go out with Richard?
Stephanie: Yeah. We went to a movie last Saturday. We saw *Police Partners II*.
Laura: Did you like it?
Stephanie: Richard did, but I didn't. Of course I told him I liked it.
Laura: Yeah. So did you do anything else?
Stephanie: Well, we went to a dance club.
Laura: Did you have fun there?
Stephanie: Yeah, we had a great time. And we're going to go there again next week.

# 7 GRAMMAR FOCUS: Past tense of irregular verbs

> **Did** you **see** any movies this weekend?
> Yes, I **did**. I **saw** *Police Partners II*.
>
> **Did** you go home after the movie?
> No, I **didn't**. I **went** to a dance club.

**1** Complete the chart on the right with the present tense (or simple) form of the verb.

**2** *Pair work* Complete the conversations with verb forms. Then practice with a partner.

A: ............... you ............... a good weekend?
B: Yes, I ............... . I ............... a great weekend.

A: ............... you ............... to a restaurant last night?
B: No, I ............... . I ............... dinner at home.

A: ............... you ............... the newspaper this morning?
B: Yes, I ............... . I ............... the newspaper before work.

A: ............... you ............... breakfast this morning?
B: Yes, I ............... . I ............... toast and tea.

| present | past | present | past |
|---|---|---|---|
| blow | blew | put | put |
| ............... | bought | read | read /red/ |
| come | came | ............... | ran |
| ............... | did | say | said |
| draw | drew | see | saw |
| drink | drank | ............... | sang |
| drive | drove | sit | sat |
| ............... | ate | ............... | slept |
| feel | felt | stand | stood |
| find | found | ............... | swam |
| get | got | take | took |
| give | gave | teach | taught |
| ............... | went | ............... | told |
| have | had | think | thought |
| know | knew | wear | wore |
| ............... | made | ............... | wrote |
| meet | met | | |

**3** *Pair work*   Choose seven questions to ask your partner.
Then take turns asking questions as in the example. Pay attention
to the forms of the verb.

☐ Did you read any books last weekend?      ☐ Did you buy any clothes?

☐ Did you write any letters?                ☐ Did you go out?

☐ Did you do any work?                       ☐ Did you see any friends?

☐ Did you exercise?                          ☐ Did you have dinner at a restaurant?

☐ Did you swim?                              ☐ Did you see any movies?

☐ Did you go skating?                        ☐ Did you go dancing?

☐ Did you go shopping?                       ☐ Did you meet any interesting people?

A: Did you read any books last weekend?
B: Yes, I did. I read *A Room With a View.*
   Did you go out?
A: No, I stayed home.

▶**Interchange 14: Past and present**

Are you different from when you were a child? Turn to page IC-17.

## 8 LISTENING 📼

Listen to four men talk about their weekends.
What did they do on Saturday morning?
Write the names under the pictures.

Philip        Mark        Chris        Matthew

.........................

.........................

.........................

.........................

# 9 READING 🔊

# A short history of the weekend

**What did you do last weekend? You probably relaxed and didn't think about work for two days. But people didn't always have two-day weekends. Where does the weekend come from?**

**2000 B.C.– 1800 A.D.** Many people spent one day a week on religion. This was called a "holy day" in England, and the English word *holiday* comes from this expression. On this day people rested and prayed.

*The Parthenon, an ancient Greek temple on the Acropolis in Athens*

**1800–1840** Sunday was the "holy" day. But many workers used this day to play games and have fun. And then they didn't go to work on Monday morning because they felt too tired. In the U.S., workers called these days "blue Mondays."

*Picnic next to a river, mid-1800s*

**1874** In England, Saturday afternoon became a holiday. Work stopped at one o'clock. This was the beginning of the weekend in England. Around 1900 in the U.S., workers began to take off Saturday afternoons in the summer. Then, by 1930, most offices were closed on Saturday afternoons all year.

*Boat trip, early 1900s*

*Family picnic, circa 1940*

**1940** Offices and factories were closed all day Saturday, and the two-day weekend began in the U.S. What did people do on those first weekends? They went to the theater or the movies. They took the train and visited their friends. They took walks in the park. They relaxed and had fun.

Read the article. Match the two parts of the sentences.

a) Before 1800, people . . .
b) In the early 1800s, workers . . .
c) In 1874, English workers . . .
d) By 1930, American workers . . .
e) After 1940, American workers . . .

1) had a two-day weekend.
2) began to take off Saturday afternoons.
3) generally rested and prayed on Sundays.
4) stopped work at one o'clock on Saturdays.
5) didn't rest on Sundays, and then felt too tired to work on Mondays.

# 15 Where were you born?

## 1 SNAPSHOT

### FAMOUS AMERICANS BORN IN OTHER COUNTRIES

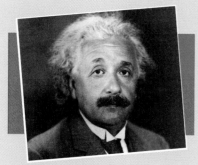

**Albert Einstein**
(1879–1955)

▶ Scientist
▶ Born in Germany
▶ Published *Theory of Relativity* in 1915

**I. M. Pei** (1917– )

▶ Architect
▶ Born in China
▶ Buildings: Pyramid in the Louvre, Paris; Bank of China in Hong Kong

**Martina Navratilova** (1956– )

▶ Tennis player
▶ Born in the former Czechoslovakia
▶ Winner of Wimbledon, 1978–79, 1982–87, 1990

Name famous people in your country who came from another country. ..............................................

## 2 CONVERSATION 📼

Listen and practice.

Chuck:   Were you born in the U.S., Melissa?
Melissa: No, I wasn't. I came here in 1992.
Chuck:   How old were you?
Melissa: I was seventeen.
Chuck:   So, did you go to college right away?
Melissa: No, because my English wasn't very good. I studied English for two years first.
Chuck:   Wow, your English is really fluent now.
Melissa: Thanks. Your English is pretty good, too.
Chuck:   Yeah, but I was born here.

# 3 YEARS 🔊

**1**  Listen and practice.

1215 (twelve fifteen)  1769 (seventeen sixty-nine)  1812 (eighteen twelve)

1906 (nineteen oh six)  1917 (nineteen seventeen)  1949 (nineteen forty-nine)

**2**  Look at the pictures of Melissa and answer the questions.

a) When was Melissa born?
b) When did she start school?
c) When did she come to the U.S.?
d) When did she enter college?

1992

1975

1980

1994

# 4 LISTENING 🔊

Where were these people born? When were they born? Listen
and complete the chart.

*Elizabeth Taylor*

*Michael J. Fox*

*Mel Gibson*

| | | | |
|---|---|---|---|
| Place of birth | .................... | .................... | .................... |
| Year of birth | .................... | .................... | .................... |

## **5** GRAMMAR FOCUS: Statements and questions with *was* and *were* 🔲

| I | **was** | born in Korea. |
|---|---------|----------------|
| He | **wasn't** | |
| She | | |
| You | **were** | born in the U.S. |
| We | **weren't** | |
| They | | |

When **were** you born?
   I **was** born in 1975.

**Were** you born in the U.S.?
   No, I **wasn't**.

**Were** your parents born in Korea?
   Yes, they **were**.

**wasn't** = was not
**weren't** = were not

**1** Complete the conversations.

A: Where _were_ you born?
B: I .................. born in Brazil.
A: .................. your parents born there, too?
B: Yes, they .................. . They .................. born in Rio.

A: When .................. your daughter born?
B: She .................. born in 1990.
A: How old .................. you then?
B: I .................. twenty-five.

A: How .................. your weekend?
B: It .................. OK.
A: .................. the weather nice?
B: No, it .................. . It rained every day.

**2** *Pair work*   Complete the questions with **was** or **were**.
Then ask and answer questions with a partner.

a) .................. you born in this city?
b) When .................. you born?
c) .................. your parents born here?
d) When .................. your mother born?
e) When .................. your father born?
f) .................. you a good student in high school?
g) What .................. your favorite subject?
h) .................. you good at sports?
i) .................. you good at languages?
j) Who .................. your first English teacher?

A: Were you born in this city?
B: No, I wasn't. I was born in Hong Kong.

CENTRAL HIGH SCHOOL
Unified School District

NAME: Gordon, Megan    YEAR: SENIOR
ACADEMIC YEAR: 1993-94

| CLASS | TEACHER | GRADE |
|-------|---------|-------|
| ENGLISH | Ms. MacLean | A |
| CALCULUS | Mr. Walton | B |
| SPANISH | Mrs. Myer | A |
| PHYSICAL EDUCATION | Mr. Renzi | B |
| GERMAN | Miss Hoffman | B |
| HISTORY | Mr. Armstrong | A |
| CHEMISTRY | Ms. Clayton | C |

# 6 PRONUNCIATION: Negative contractions 📟

**1** Listen and practice.

| *one syllable* | *two syllables* |
|---|---|
| aren't | isn't |
| weren't | wasn't |
| don't | doesn't |
| | didn't |

**2** Practice these sentences.

I **didn't** see them because they **weren't** there.
He **isn't** here because he **wasn't** well.
She **doesn't** know that we **aren't** home.

# 7 CONVERSATION 📟

Listen and practice.

Melissa: How about you, Chuck?
Where did you grow up?
Chuck: Well, I was born in Ohio,
but I grew up in Texas.
Melissa: And when did you come to
Los Angeles?
Chuck: In 1978. I went to college here.
Melissa: Oh. What was your major?
Chuck: Drama. I was an actor for
five years after college.
Melissa: That's interesting. So why did you
become a hairdresser?
Chuck: Because I needed the money. And
because I was good at it. Look.
What do you think?

## 8 GRAMMAR FOCUS: Wh-questions with *did, was,* and *were*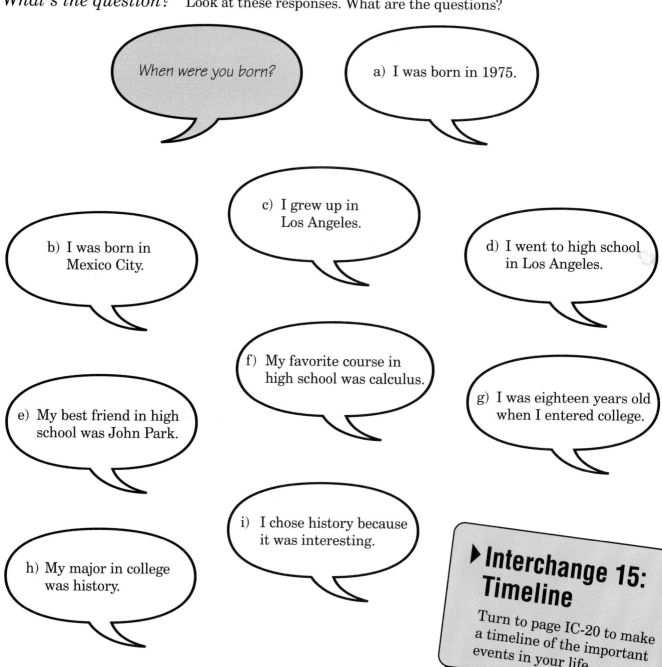

**Where** did you grow up?      I grew up **in Texas**.
**Why** did you become a hairdresser?      I became a hairdresser **because I needed the money**.
**When** did you come to Los Angeles?      I came to L.A. **in 1978**.

**How old** were you in 1978?      I was **eighteen**.
**What** was your major in college?      It was **drama**.
**Who** was your first friend in L.A.?      My first friend was **Bob Rivers**.
**How** was your vacation?      It was **great**.

*What's the question?*    Look at these responses. What are the questions?

When were you born?

a) I was born in 1975.

c) I grew up in Los Angeles.

b) I was born in Mexico City.

d) I went to high school in Los Angeles.

f) My favorite course in high school was calculus.

e) My best friend in high school was John Park.

g) I was eighteen years old when I entered college.

i) I chose history because it was interesting.

h) My major in college was history.

▶ **Interchange 15: Timeline**

Turn to page IC-20 to make a timeline of the important events in your life.

# 9 READING 📼

**1** Read about these people in the paragraphs below. Match the people with the paragraphs.

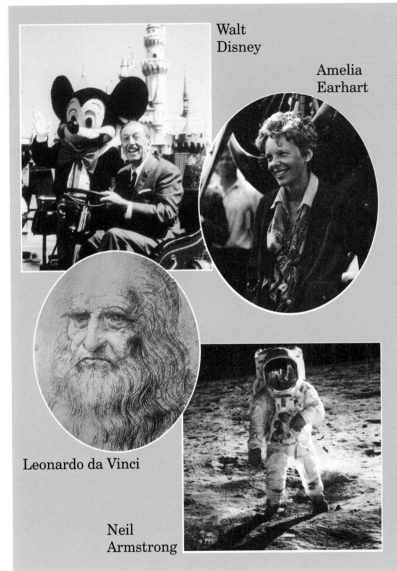

Walt Disney

Amelia Earhart

Leonardo da Vinci

Neil Armstrong

## Some famous people

.......................... This Italian painter lived from 1452 to 1519. In about 1504 he painted the *Mona Lisa*, the most famous painting in the world. The *Mona Lisa* is now in the Louvre Museum in Paris. It was stolen in 1911, but it was found again two years later.

.......................... In 1928 this aviator became the first woman to fly across the Atlantic Ocean as a passenger. In 1932 she completed a solo transatlantic flight. She also tried to fly around the world, but she disappeared over the Pacific in 1937.

.......................... This artist and film producer was the creator of Mickey Mouse. Mickey Mouse's first animated cartoon appeared in 1928. Mickey Mouse soon became the world's most popular animated cartoon character, and he received over 2,000 letters a day.

.......................... This astronaut was the first human to walk on the moon. He stepped onto the moon on July 20, 1969. He said, "That's one small step for man, one giant leap for mankind."

**2** Complete the chart.

| Name | Profession | One important thing he or she did | Date |
|------|-----------|-----------------------------------|------|
| Walt Disney | .................... | ................................................................ | ............ |
| .................... | .................... | ................................................................ | ............ |
| .................... | .................... | ................................................................ | ............ |
| .................... | .................... | ................................................................ | ............ |

**3** Write a few sentences about a famous person from your country.

# 16 Hello. Is Jennifer there, please?

## 1 SNAPSHOT

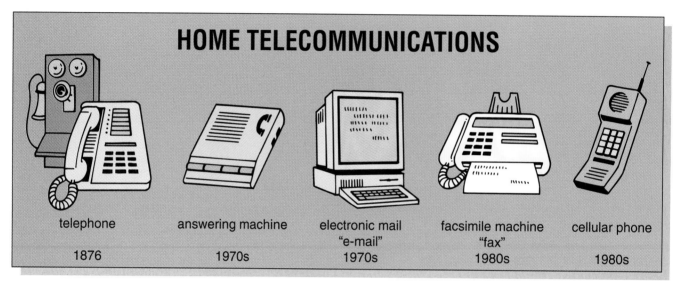

**HOME TELECOMMUNICATIONS**

| telephone | answering machine | electronic mail "e-mail" | facsimile machine "fax" | cellular phone |
|-----------|-------------------|--------------------------|-------------------------|----------------|
| 1876 | 1970s | 1970s | 1980s | 1980s |

What telecommunications equipment do you have at home? ...........................................................

What equipment do you want? ...........................................................

## 2 CONVERSATION

**1** Listen and practice.

Tracy: Hello?

Michael: Hi, Tracy. This is Michael. Is Jennifer there?

Tracy: I'm sorry, Michael, she's at her parents' house. She's having dinner with them. Do you want to leave her a message?

Michael: Oh, I'm not sure. It's a little complicated.

Tracy: I have an idea. I'm going out now. So call again and leave her a message on the machine.

Michael: That's a good idea.

Tracy: And don't worry, I'm not going to listen to it.

Michael: Thanks, Tracy. You're a real pal.

**2** Now listen to Michael's message. Why did he call Jennifer?

# 3 PLACES 📼

**1** Listen and practice.

*Jennifer isn't here right now . . .*

She's **at** work.
   **at** class.
   **at** the pool.
   **at** her parents' house.
   **at** the office.
   **at** the mall.

She's **in** South America.
   **in** the hospital.

She's **on** vacation.
   **on** a trip.

*at the mall*

*Jennifer can't come to the phone right now . . .*

She's **in** bed.
   **in** the shower.

She's **on** the roof.

*on the roof*

**2** *Pair work* Make a telephone call and ask for one of the people below. Your partner tells you where the person is.

A: Hello, is ............ there, please?
B: I'm sorry, he can't come to the phone right now. He's . . .
   (She's not here right now. She's . . . )

**Michael**

**Brian**

**Victor**

**Lisa**

**Sarah**

**Nicole**

## 4 | GRAMMAR FOCUS: Subject and object pronouns 🔲

| | me | | I | |
|---|---|---|---|---|
| | you | | you | |
| They left | her | a message, but | she | didn't get it. |
| | him | | he | |
| | us | | we | |
| | them | | they | |

*Pair work*   Complete these telephone conversations with pronouns.
Then practice with a partner.

A: Is Robert there, please?
B: ................... 'm sorry, ................... 's not here right now.
   Do ................... want to leave ................... a message?
A: Yes, this is David. Please tell ................... to call ................... at work.
B: Can ................... tell ................... your phone number there?
A: Sure, ................... 's 555-2981.

A: Can ................... speak with Mr. Ford, please?
B: ................... 's not in today. But maybe ................... can help ................... .
A: Can ................... tell ................... to call John Rivers?
B: John Rivers. OK. Does ................... have your number?
A: Yes, ................... 'm sure he has ................... .

A: This is the answering machine for Tom and Bill.
   Please leave ................... a message after the tone.
B: Bill, this is Maria. ................... left your hat and gloves here yesterday.
   If ................... need ................... , come and pick ................... up this evening.
   Hey, ................... love your hat. Where did you buy ................... ?

## 5 | CONVERSATION 🔲

Listen and practice.

Michael:   Hello?
Jennifer:  Hello, Michael. This is Jennifer.
           I got your message.
Michael:   Great. So, do you want to go to
           the movies on Thursday?
Jennifer:  I'm really sorry, but I can't.
           I have to stay home and study.
Michael:   That's too bad.
Jennifer:  You know, I'm having a little
           party next Saturday. Do you
           want to come?
Michael:   That sounds great. What time
           does it start?
Jennifer:  Around eight o'clock.
Michael:   OK. See you then.

# 6  GRAMMAR FOCUS: Verb + *to* + verb 🔲

| Do you **want to go** to the movies? | Do you **have to stay** home? | Do you **like to go** to parties? |
| --- | --- | --- |
| I **want to go** to the movies. | I **have to stay** home on Thursday. | Of course I **like to go** to parties. |
| I don't **want to stay** home. | I **need to study**. | |

**1**  Complete these conversations with **have to**, **need to**, **like to**, or **want to**. Then practice with a partner.

A: This is a beautiful hat. I ............... buy it.
B: Please don't buy it. We ............... save money.

A: I love Chinese, and I ............... speak it fluently.
B: Then you ............... study very hard. It's a difficult language.

A: Do you ............... go dancing tonight?
B: I really ............... go, but I can't. I ............... work late.

A: I ............... work this Saturday, so let's go to the beach.
B: That sounds great. But we ............... clean the house first.

A: Do you ............... go to a party next Friday?
B: Thanks, but I don't ............... go to parties.

**2**  *Pair work*  Write answers to these questions. Then compare with a partner.

a) What are three things you have to do this week?
b) What are three things you need to buy this month?
c) What are three things you like to do on the weekend?
d) What are three things you want to learn this year?

*Drawing by Eric Teitelbaum; © 1994 The New Yorker Magazine, Inc.*

---

# 7  PRONUNCIATION: *want to, have to* 🔲

**1**  Listen and practice. Notice the pronunciation of **want to** and **have to**.

/wanə/

I **want to** see a movie.
I **want to** go home.

/hæftə/

I **have to** meet a friend.
I **have to** work late.

**2**  *Pair work*  Practice the conversations in exercise 1 of the Grammar Focus again. Pay attention to **want to** and **have to**.

## 8 EXCUSES

**1** *Pair work* How often do you use these excuses? Check **often**, **sometimes**, or **never**. What are your three favorite excuses? Compare with a partner.

|  | often | sometimes | never |
|---|:---:|:---:|:---:|
| I have to work late. | ☐ | ☐ | ☐ |
| I have to study. | ☐ | ☐ | ☐ |
| I have to go to bed early. | ☐ | ☐ | ☐ |
| I have to save money. | ☐ | ☐ | ☐ |
| I'm going to visit my parents. | ☐ | ☐ | ☐ |
| I'm going to go to a lecture. | ☐ | ☐ | ☐ |
| I have a terrible headache. | ☐ | ☐ | ☐ |
| I have a terrible backache. | ☐ | ☐ | ☐ |
| I want to stay home and watch television. | ☐ | ☐ | ☐ |
| I want to stay home and read. | ☐ | ☐ | ☐ |

**2** *Class activity* Write down three places you want to go this weekend. Choose a specific day and time. Then invite classmates to go with you.

A: Do you want to .................... on .................... ?
B: I'm sorry, but I can't. I have to .................... .
A: Do you want to .................... on .................... ?
B: That sounds great. When do you want to meet?

▶ **Interchange 16: Let's make a date**
Student A turns to page IC-19 and Student B turns to page IC-21. Check your calendar and make a date!

## 9 LISTENING 🔊

**1** Jennifer invited friends to a party on Saturday. Listen to the messages on her answering machine. Who can come? Who can't come?

|  | can come | can't come |
|---|:---:|:---:|
| Kumiko | ☐ | ☐ |
| David | ☐ | ☐ |
| Sarah | ☐ | ☐ |
| Victor | ☐ | ☐ |
| Nicole | ☐ | ☐ |

**2** Listen again. For those who can't come, what reason do they give?

| name | reason |
|---|---|
| ................................ | ................................ |
| ................................ | ................................ |

## 10 READING 🔲

### FREE ACTIVITIES THIS WEEKEND

**CITY MUSEUM TRAVEL SERIES**
If you want to travel, but don't have enough money, see movies on Japan, Indonesia, Brazil, Italy, and Australia. Saturday and Sunday at 2:30 P.M. There are only 100 seats in the theater, so come early.

### CANINE CLUB SHOW
County Fairgrounds, Saturday at 2:00 P.M. 100 dogs of all shapes and sizes show their talents. Come and vote for the best dog. No cats, please. Sandwiches and soda sold at the show.

### ROCK CONCERT AT UNIVERSITY PARK
Do you want to hear some great music? Five student bands are going to play at University Park Saturday evening from 9:00 P.M. to midnight. Bring your own food and drink.

### LIBRARY LECTURE SERIES
**"How to find the job you really want."**
Two-hour lecture. Advice on choosing and getting the right job for you. City Library Auditorium, Saturday at 10:00 A.M. Coffee and rolls provided.

### SUMMER FASHION SHOW
Golden Shopping Plaza, Sunday at 3:00 P.M. Men's and women's swimwear and summer wear. See 25 fabulous models in the latest fashions. All clothing on sale after the show for under $50.

**CRAFTS FAIR**
Need to buy a present for your mother, husband, or boss? Come to a crafts fair in front of City Hall on Sunday from 9:00 A.M. to 5:00 P.M. Find pottery, jewelry, paintings, sculpture, etc., and food from around the world.

**1** Read the article. Then write down two activities where you can . . .

a) buy clothes or jewelry .......... ..........    c) sit indoors .......... ..........
b) buy food .......... ..........    d) be outdoors .......... ..........

**2** *Pair work*  List three things you want to do. Then compare with a partner. Find one activity you can do together.

First choice: ..........
Second choice: ..........
Third choice: ..........

# Review of Units 13-16

## 1 Classroom rules

Write down four things you have to do in class.
Write down four things you can't do in class.
Compare with a partner.

> *You have to listen to the teacher . . .*
> *You can't smoke . . .*

## 2 Locations

**1** *Pair work*   Take turns giving the location of these places. Give the location in two different ways.

a) parking lot
b) drugstore
c) night club
d) bus stop
e) public restroom

A: The parking lot is on Second Avenue.
B: The parking lot is across from the Korean restaurant.

**2** *Pair work*   Give directions to two different places on the map. Your partner guesses the destination.

A: Walk up First Avenue and turn left. It's on the right, on the corner of First and Lincoln.
B: It's the Japanese restaurant.
A: Right.

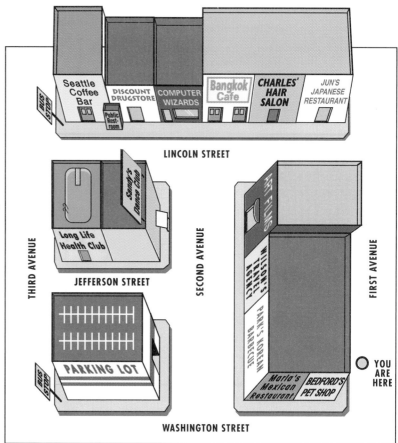

## 3 No, she wasn't!

**1** *Class activity*   Write three false statements about famous people in the past. Read your sentences to the class. Can anyone correct them?

> *Marilyn Monroe was a famous tennis player.*
> *Elvis Presley . . .*

A: Marilyn Monroe was a famous tennis player.
B: No, she wasn't. She was a movie star.

# 4 Tell us about it

*Group work*   Tell your classmates some of the things you did
last week. Each student then asks one question about it.

Tell them about . . .

a) something you did last week that you liked.
b) something you did last week that you didn't like.
c) someone interesting who you talked to last week.
d) something interesting that you bought last week.

A: I saw a movie last week.
B: What was the name of the movie?  . . .
C: Who was in it? . . .
D: How did you like it? . . .

# 5 Listening 🔲

Listen and choose the correct response.

a) ☐ No, they weren't.
   ☐ No, they aren't.

b) ☐ At eleven o'clock.
   ☐ No, I didn't.

c) ☐ We took the bus.
   ☐ Amy and Katherine.

d) ☐ It was great.
   ☐ Sue and Tom were.

e) ☐ I'm going to visit my parents on Sunday.
   ☐ Because I had a terrible headache.

f) ☐ I'm sorry, but I can't. I have to work.
   ☐ No, I didn't go. I was at work.

g) ☐ I'm sorry, he's not here right now.
   ☐ Stephanie is at work right now.

h) ☐ There's a restaurant on Grant Street.
   ☐ No, there isn't. Sorry.

# 6 Future plans

Make a list of five things you want to do in the
next five years. Then compare with a partner.

> I want to find a wife (husband).
> I want to get a job in a bank.

# Interchange Activities

**Planning a picnic**

*Useful expressions*

What's your favorite . . . ?
My favorite . . . is . . .
What foods don't you like?
I like . . ./I don't like . . .

**1** *Group work*   Plan a picnic with some friends.
First, find out what foods people like and don't like to eat.
Complete the chart.

| Name | | | | |
|---|---|---|---|---|
| Three favorite picnic foods | .......................... .......................... .......................... | .......................... .......................... .......................... | .......................... .......................... .......................... | .......................... .......................... .......................... |
| Favorite drink | .......................... | .......................... | .......................... | .......................... |
| Favorite dessert | .......................... | .......................... | .......................... | .......................... |
| Foods or drink he/she doesn't like | .......................... .......................... | .......................... .......................... | .......................... .......................... | .......................... .......................... |

**2**   Now make a menu for the picnic. Choose three foods,
two drinks, and one dessert.

*Useful expressions*

Let's have . . .
Juan doesn't want . . .
Everyone likes . . .

*Picnic menu*

..............................................
..............................................
..............................................
..............................................
..............................................
..............................................
..............................................
..............................................

**3** *Class activity*   Compare
menus with the rest of the class.

IC–12

## Interchange 10  Hidden talents

**1** *Class activity*  Walk around the class asking questions to fill in the chart below. Find one person who **can** and one person who **can't** do each thing.

A: Can you touch your toes?
B: Yes I can.  (No, I can't.)

| Can you . . . | **can** (name) | **can't** (name) |
|---|---|---|
| 1. touch your toes? | | |
| 2. play a musical instrument? | | |
| 3. dance the tango? | | |
| 4. say "Hello" in 5 different languages? | | |
| 5. swim underwater? | | |
| 6. remember lots of telephone numbers? | | |
| 7. write with both hands? | | |
| 8. sing a song in English? | | |
| 9. ride a horse? | | |
| 10. juggle? | | |
| 11. make your own clothes? | | |
| 12. do magic tricks? | | |

*riding a horse*

*juggling*

*doing magic tricks*

**2**  Report your results to the class.

*Noriko can't touch her toes, but she knows how to juggle.*

## Interchange 11 | Vacation plans

**1** *Pair work*   Answer questions about vacation plans, or talk about your "dream" vacation. Then ask about your partner's plans.

| | Me | My partner |
|---|---|---|
| 1. When is your next vacation? | .......................... | .......................... |
| 2. How long are you going to be on vacation? | .......................... | .......................... |

April   August
July   December

for one week   for two weeks   for a long weekend   for one month

3. Where are you going to go?
4. What are you going to do?

5. How are you going to go?
6. Who are you going to go with?

7. What are you going to eat?
8. What are you going to bring back?

GUIDE BOOK

**2** *Group work*   Two pairs form a group. Tell the group your partner's plans.

"Maria's next vacation is in July. She's going to be on vacation for one week . . ."

## Interchange 12  Helpful advice

**1** *Pair work*  Look at the problems below. Give advice to each person.

> I want to lose a little weight, but I really like desserts. Ice cream is my favorite food!

> My job is very stressful. I usually work 10 hours a day and on weekends. I have backaches and headaches almost every day.

> I can never get up on time in the morning. I'm always late for work. I guess I'm not a morning person.

> I'm new in town and I don't know any people here. I want to make some friends.

**2** *Class activity*  Write down two problems that you have. Then tell the class. Your classmates give you advice.

> I can't sleep at night . . .

A: I can't sleep at night.
B: Get up and do some work.
C: Don't drink coffee in the evening.

# Interchange 13 Directions – STUDENT A

*Pair work*

**1**  Look at the map. You are on Third Avenue between Maple and Oak Streets. Ask your partner for directions to:

a) a car wash          b) a supermarket          c) a flower shop

Mark the location on the map.

A: Excuse me. Is there a car wash near here?
B: Yes, there is. It's . . .

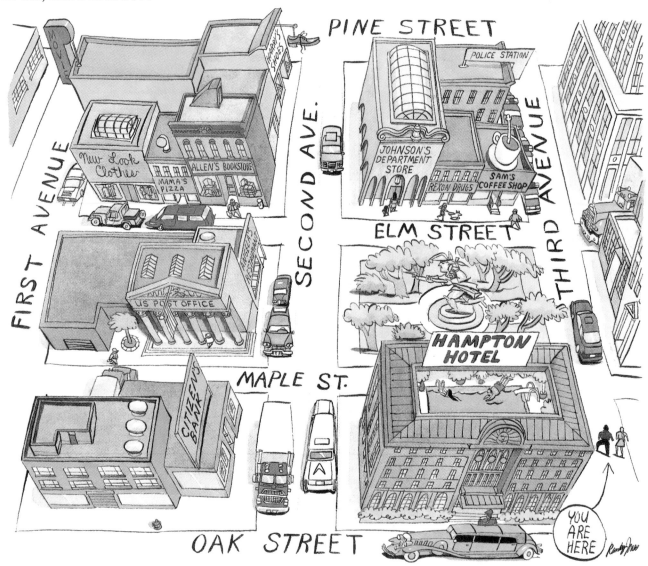

**2**  Now your partner asks you for directions to three places. Give your partner directions, using the expressions in the box.

*Useful expressions*

| | | |
|---|---|---|
| Go right/left . . . | It's on the corner of . . . Street and . . . Avenue | It's next to . . . |
| Walk one block . . . | It's between . . . and . . . | It's behind . . . |
| Turn right/left . . . | It's across from . . . | It's in front of . . . |

# Interchange 14 | Past and present

**1** *Pair work* Ask a partner questions about the past and about the present. Write down the answers.

A: As a child, did you clean your room?
B: Yes, I did. (No, I didn't.)
A: Do you clean your room now?
B: Yes I do. (No, I don't.)

## Did you . . . as a child?
## Do you . . . now?

*making a bed*

| | as a child | now |
|---|---|---|
| 1. make your own bed? | ............ | ............ |
| 2. clean your room? | ............ | ............ |
| 3. wake up early? | ............ | ............ |
| 4. sleep late on Saturdays? | ............ | ............ |
| 5. fight with your friends? | ............ | ............ |
| 6. argue with your family? | ............ | ............ |
| 7. listen to rock music? | ............ | ............ |
| 8. listen to classical music? | ............ | ............ |
| 9. use a computer? | ............ | ............ |
| 10. play video games? | ............ | ............ |
| 11. play a musical instrument? | ............ | ............ |
| 12. play a sport? | ............ | ............ |
| 13. wear glasses? | ............ | ............ |
| 14. wear braces? | ............ | ............ |
| 15. have a stamp collection? | ............ | ............ |

*collecting stamps*

*wearing braces*

*fighting with a friend*

**2** *Group work* Join with another pair. Tell them about your partner.

"Tai-lin didn't clean his room as a child, but he does now."

## Interchange 13 | Directions – STUDENT B

*Pair work*

**1**   Look at the map. You are on Third Avenue between Maple and
Oak Streets. Your partner asks you for directions to three places.
Give your partner directions using the expressions in the box.

| *Useful expressions* | | |
|---|---|---|
| Go right/left . . . | It's on the corner of . . . Street and . . . Avenue | It's next to . . . |
| Walk one block . . . | It's between . . . and . . . | It's behind . . . |
| Turn right/left . . . | It's across from . . . | It's in front of . . . |

A: Excuse me. Is there a car wash near here?
B: Yes, there is. It's . . .

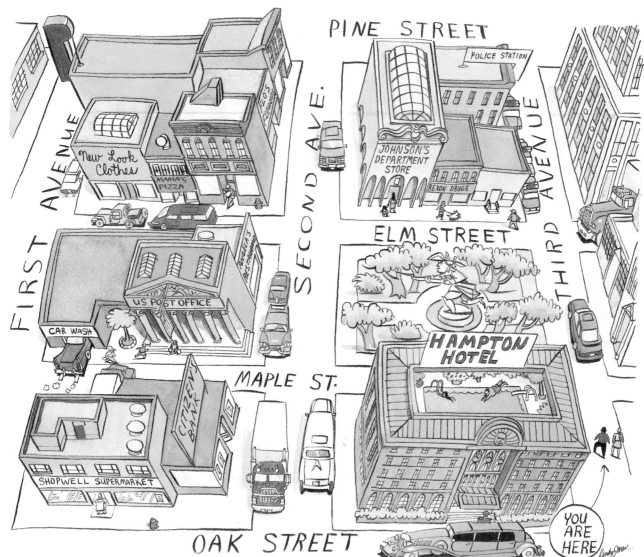

**2**   Now ask your partner for directions to:

a) a coffee shop        b) a shoe store        c) a bookstore

Mark the location on the map.

## Interchange 16 | Let's make a date – STUDENT A

*Pair work*

**1** This is your calendar for March. You want to make an evening date with Student B. Ask and answer questions to find out when you are both free. Follow this conversation.

A: Do you want to go out on March third?
B: I want to, but I can't. I have to go ice-skating with Marie.

Continue until you find a date.

| Sunday | Monday | Tuesday | Wednesday | Thursday | Friday | Saturday |
|---|---|---|---|---|---|---|
| **1** visit my parents | **2** go to my tennis class | **3** | **4** go to the dentist | **5** | **6** have dinner with Charles | **7** |
| **8** | **9** go to my tennis class | **10** | **11** go dancing at the Hard Rock Cafe | **12** | **13** | **14** go to Bill's birthday party – present: CD? |
| **15** vacation! | **16** | **17** | **18** | **19** | **20** | **21** |
| **22** | **23** go to my tennis class | **24** | **25** meet David, Linda, and Tracy | **26** | **27** | **28** |
| **29** go out with Chris's friend (name?!) | **30** | **31** go to the movies with Jane | *March* | | | |

**2** Now that you have a date, you need to decide what to do. Discuss the possibilities. Use this conversation as a guide.

A: Do you want to play tennis?
B: No, I'm not very good at tennis. Do you want to go ice-skating?
A: No, I don't know how to ice-skate.

Continue until you decide what to do. Then tell the class your plan.

## Interchange 15 | Timeline

*Pair work*

**1**  What are five important events in your life? Mark them on the timeline below and write a sentence about each one.

*I was born in 1970.*

1950   1960   1970   1980   1990   2000

I was born . . .

I graduated from high school . . .

I got married . . .

My first child was born . . .

**2**  Find out the five important years in your partner's life. Tell your partner your five important years. Ask and answer questions.

A:  What happened in 1990?
B:  I met my wife.
A:  How did you meet her?

## Interchange 16 | Let's make a date – STUDENT B

*Pair work*

**1**  This is your calendar for March. You want to make an evening date with Student A. Ask and answer questions to find out when you are both free. Follow this conversation.

A: Do you want to go out on March third?
B: I want to, but I can't. I have to go ice-skating with Marie.

Continue until you find a date.

| Sunday | Monday | Tuesday | Wednesday | Thursday | Friday | Saturday |
|---|---|---|---|---|---|---|
| **1** | **2** | **3** go ice-skating with Marie | **4** have dinner with Sue – Thai restaurant? | **5** go to my guitar lesson | **6** | **7** see a movie with Joe |
| **8** visit my parents | **9** | **10** go swimming with Michiko | **11** | **12** go to my guitar lesson | **13** go to the Billy Joel concert | **14** |
| **15** | **16** go to Frank's party | **17** have dinner with Carlos | **18** | **19** go to my guitar lesson | **20** | **21** |
| **22** vacation | **23** | **24** | **25** | **26** go to my guitar lesson | **27** visit my grand-parents | **28** |
| **29** | **30** go shopping with my parents | **31** | | | | |

# March

**2**  Now that you have a date, you need to decide what to do. Discuss the possibilities. Use this conversation as a guide.

A: Do you want to play tennis?
B: No, I'm not very good at tennis. Do you want to go ice-skating?
A: No, I don't know how to ice-skate.

Continue until you decide what to do. Then tell the class your plan.

# Key Vocabulary

## Unit 9  I love strawberries!

### NOUNS

**Dairy**
butter
cheese
egg(s)*
milk
yogurt

**Desserts**
cake
chocolate
cookie(s)
ice cream
pie (apple pie)

**Drinks**
lemonade
milk
soda
tea (green tea)

**Fish**
salmon
shrimp

**Fruit**
apple(s)
banana(s)
mango (mangoes)
orange(s)
strawberry
  (strawberries)

**Meat**
bacon
beef
chicken
hamburger (meat)
hot dog(s)
lamb

**Starches**
bean(s)
bread
bun(s)
pasta
potato (potatoes)
rice

**Vegetables**
bean(s)
broccoli
carrot(s)
celery
green bean(s)
onion(s)
pepper(s)
tomato (tomatoes)

**Other foods**
mayonnaise
potato salad
salad
sandwich(es)
snack(s)
toast

**Other nouns**
barbecue
freezer
meal
picnic

*Plurals are given here
for foods that are
countable nouns.

### VERBS
buy
choose
drink
eat
hate
love

love to
make
need to
think
try
want

### ADVERBS
always
ever
never
often

seldom
sometimes
usually

### ADJECTIVES
awful
delicious
Japanese-style
same
traditional

### PRONOUN
everyone

### EXPRESSIONS

. . . is / are good for you.
How about some . . . ?
Let's not . . .
We need to buy . . .
I have . . . for breakfast.

Why don't you . . . ?
I love to try new things.
To make a sandwich, you need . . .

## Unit 10  Can you swim very well?

### NOUNS

**Sports**
baseball
basketball
football
golf
Ping-Pong
skating
  (ice-skating)
skiing
soccer
swimming
tennis
volleyball
team sport
individual sport

**Games**
board game
card game
chess
video game

**Other nouns**
date
girlfriend
lap (of a pool)
poetry
pool
sport

### VERBS
can / can't
cook
dance
dive
draw
fix (a car)
have (a date)
know how to
play (a game)
play (a sport)
play (the piano)
sing
skate (ice-skate)
ski

### ADVERBS
at all
even
fluently
quite well
too / either
(not) very well

### ADJECTIVES
late
terrific

### EXPRESSIONS
I can't even . . .
I can teach you how to . . .
In fact . . .
Wow!
What's that?
I know how to . . .
I'm good at . . .
There's one thing
  (that) . . .
She's not good at
  remembering things.
She's an hour late!

# Unit 11  When's your birthday?

| NOUNS | | VERBS | ADVERBS | EXPRESSIONS |
|---|---|---|---|---|
| birthday | place | blow out (candles) | next week (month, year, | I hope so. |
| birthday cake | present | celebrate | summer, Saturday, etc.) | Nice! |
| candles | speech | kiss | probably | How old are you? |
| day | year | order | tomorrow | I'm . . . years old. |
| diploma | | receive | tomorrow night | I bet . . . |
| fireworks | *Months* | shout | tonight | It's going to be fun. |
| friend | *(See page 68.)* | | | Happy Birthday! |
| fun | | | | Happy New Year! |
| graduation | | | | have a good time |
| holiday | | | | |
| month | | | | |
| party | | | | |

| ADJECTIVES | | WH-WORD |
|---|---|---|
| embarrassing | *Ordinal* | How old |
| next | *numbers* | |
| special | *(See page 68.)* | |

# Unit 12  What's the matter?

| NOUNS | | |
|---|---|---|
| *Body parts* | shoulder | *Other nouns* |
| arm | stomach | appointment |
| back | tooth *(pl* teeth) | aspirin |
| ear | *Illnesses* | bath |
| eye | backache | exercise |
| foot *(pl* feet) | cold | opening |
| hand | earache | pill |
| head | fever | place |
| leg | (the) flu | (=residence) |
| mouth | headache | water |
| neck | sore throat | |
| nose | stomachache | |

| ADJECTIVES | | | | |
|---|---|---|---|---|
| bad | every | free | sad | terrible |
| better | fine | heavy | sore | |

**EXPRESSIONS**

How are you?
I'm fine.
That's fine.
I'm just feeling a little sad.
I don't think so.
Listen.
Thanks a lot.
How do you feel?
What's wrong?
That's too bad.
I hope you feel better soon.
I'm sorry to hear that.

I have a headache (a stomachache, a cold, the flu, a sore throat, sore eyes, etc.).
Hello, this is . . .
Can I make an appointment?
Take these pills every four hours.
I have trouble remembering . . .
When is . . . again?
Go home.
Go to bed. / Stay in bed.

| VERBS | | ADVERBS | |
|---|---|---|---|
| feel (sad) | lose (weight) | a little | just |
| forget | relax | already | soon |
| get (exercise) | sit down | early | then |
| go out | take (a bath) | | |
| lift | take (a pill) | | |

# Unit 13  Can you help me, please?

| NOUNS | | VERBS | ADJECTIVES | EXPRESSIONS |
|---|---|---|---|---|
| *Places* | post office | get (to a place) | expensive | Can you help me, please? |
| bookstore | restroom | look up | far | Is there a . . . near here? |
| building | supermarket | turn | | Is . . . far from here? |
| bus stop | | turn around | | It's right behind you. |
| department | *Other nouns* | | **PREPOSITIONS** | Oh, no! |
| store | block | | across from | You're welcome. |
| drugstore | gasoline | **ADVERBS** | down | How do I get to . . . ? |
| gas station | magazine | left / right | on the corner of | |
| hotel | stamp | on the left / right | up | |
| newsstand | | indoors / outdoors | | |
| parking lot | | right (=exactly) | | |

# Unit 14  Did you have a good weekend?

| NOUNS | VERBS | | ADJECTIVE | EXPRESSIONS |
|---|---|---|---|---|
| activity | exercise | sleep | tired | Sort of. |
| computer | give | study | | Of course . . . |
| computer game | go dancing | take off (time ) | | That sounds like fun. |
| dance club | go shopping | tell | | Yeah. |
| letter | go skating | visit | **PREPOSITION** | Did you have fun? |
| video | hike | wash (clothes) | | We had a great time. |
| weekend | invite | | before | |
| | listen (to) | *Irregular past* | | |
| | make | *(See page 91.)* | | |
| | miss | | | |
| | rent | | | |

# Unit 15  Where were you born?

| NOUNS | VERBS | ADJECTIVES | WH-WORDS | EXPRESSIONS |
|---|---|---|---|---|
| actor | be born | best | when | Where were you born? |
| calculus | become (*past* became) | fluent | why | I was born in Korea. |
| college | choose (*past* chose) | pretty good | | I went to college |
| course | enter (college) | | | I needed the money. |
| drama | get married | | **CONJUNCTION** | Look. |
| (best) friend | graduate | | because | What do you think? |
| hairdresser | grow up (*past* grew up) | | | |
| high school | happen | | | |
| major | | | | |
| subject | **ADVERBS** | | **PREPOSITION** | |
| | right away    pretty | | after | |
| | early          (=quite) | | | |

# Unit 16   Hello. Is Jennifer there, please?

| NOUNS | | VERBS | PRONOUNS | | EXPRESSIONS |
|---|---|---|---|---|---|
| *Places* | *Other nouns* | call | I | me | I have an idea. |
| beach | idea | get (a message) | you | you | Don't worry. |
| hospital | guitar | leave (a message) | she | her | You're a real pal. |
| mall | grandparent | pick up | he | him | I'm sorry, but I can't. |
| office | lecture | save (money) | it | it | You know, . . . |
| roof | (answering) | stay (home) | we | us | Around (eight o'clock). |
| shower |    machine | have to | they | them | |
| yard | message | like to | | | *Telephone language* |
| | pal | need to | | | Is Jennifer there? |
| | party | want to | | | She isn't here right now. |
| | rock music | | | | She can't come to the |
| | trip | | | |    phone right now. |
| | | **ADVERBS** | | | Do you want to leave |
| **ADJECTIVES** | | again | **PREPOSITIONS** | |    (her) a message? |
| complicated | real | at class | around | | Leave (her) a message |
| little | sure | at home | at | |    on the machine. |
| | | early | | | |
| | | on vacation | | | |

# Acknowledgments

## Text Credits

**61** *Profiles,* in-flight magazine by Virgin Atlantic Airlines, Summer 1993; *Panati's Extraordinary Origins of Everyday Things*, HarperCollins, 1989.
**62** *(Snapshot) World Almanac and Book of Facts, 1994.*
**79** *Having Our Say: The Delany Sisters' First Hundred Years*, Kodansha, 1993; "Secrets of a Long Life from Two Who Ought to Know," *The New York Times,* September 18, 1993, p. B1.
**88** *(Snapshot)* Leisure Trends compilation of Gallup data.
**93** Adapted from Witold Rybczynski, *Waiting for the Weekend,* Penguin Books, 1991.
**95** *The 1994 Information Please Almanac*
**99** *Webster's College Encyclopedia,* Prentice-Hall, 1993.

## Illustrators

Randy Jones 72, 77, 86, 94, 95, 97, IC–13, IC–14, IC–16, IC–18
Mark Kaufman 56, 61, 80, 82, 84
Beth McNally 64 *(top)*
Wally Neibart 70, 75, 78, 85 *(top)*, 90
Bill Thomson 58, 60, 74, 83, 89, 100, 101, 102, 104
Sam Viviano 62, 63, 64 *(bottom)*, 69, 71, 76, 85 *(bottom)*, 91, 92, 107
Snapshots by Phil Scheuer

## Photographic Credits

The author and publisher are grateful for permission to reproduce the following photographs.

**57** ©1991 Mark Harmel/FPG International
**58** and **59** Noreen O'Connor-Abel
**65** *(top row, left to right)* © Jeffrey W. Myers/The Stock Market; SuperStock; © 1991 Mike Valeri/FPG International; © Kevin Michael Daly/The Stock Market; *(second row, left to right)* © Steve Brown, Sporting Pictures (UK) Ltd/Leo de Wys, Inc.; © Anne-Marie Weber/The Stock Market; © Stephen Simpson/FPG International
**66** *(top to bottom)* Noreen O'Connor-Abel; Noreen O'Connor-Abel; Howard G. Ross/FPG International; © Ken Straiton/The Stock Market
**67** *(left to right)* © T. Quing/FPG International; © Lee Kuhn/FPG International; © 1990 A. Schmidecker/FPG International
**73** *(clockwise from left)* SuperStock; David Young

Wolff/PhotoEdit; © Harvey Lloyd/The Stock Market; © Bill Wassman/The Stock Market
**75** *(ear)* Tif Hunter/Tony Stone Images; *(all others)* © 1994 Erika Stone
**79** Photograph by Brian Douglas. From *Having Our Say,* by Sarah and A. Elizabeth Delany with Amy Hill Hearth. Published by Kodansha America Inc. © Amy Hill Hearth, Sarah Louise Delany, and Annie Elizabeth Delany.
**82** FPG International; © 1992 Richard Laird/FPG International; © R. Lord/The Image Works; © Jose Luis Banus – March 1991/FPG International; Jeffrey Sylvester/FPG International; Jon Levy/Liaison; Research Photogs/FPG International; © 1991 John Medere/The Stock Market
**87** *(clockwise from top left)* © 1988 Naoki Okamato/The Stock Market; © 1991 Vladimir Pcholkin/FPG International; © Dan Lecca/FPG International; Noreen O'Connor-Abel
**93** *(clockwise from top left)* Archive Photos; The Bettmann Archive; Archive Photos/Camerique; H. Armstrong Roberts
**94** *(left to right)* Historical Pictures Service, Chicago; UPI/Bettmann; Georges De Keerle © Gamma Liaison
**95** *(left to right)* Reuters/Bettmann; UPI/Bettmann Newsphotos; © 1992 Warner Bros./SuperStock
**99** *(clockwise from top left)* Gamma Liaison; © Holmes-Lebel 1932/FPG International; Archive Photos/Lambert; SuperStock
**105** *(clockwise from top left)* J. S. Dorl/Pure Bred Dogs/*American Kennel Gazette*; Reuters/Bettmann; © Richard Danoff/The Stock Market
**IC–12** © 1992 Jon Feingersh/The Stock Market
**IC–15** *(clockwise from top left)* © Daemmrich/Stock Boston; © 1992 Jon Feingersh/The Stock Market; © 1991 Michael Krasowitz/FPG International; Mark Lewis/Tony Stone Images
**IC–17** *(clockwise from top left)* Stephen McBrady/PhotoEdit; © 1993 Ariel Skelly/The Stock Market; © 1991 Lawrence Migdale/Stock Boston; © Edward Lettau/FPG International
**IC–20** *(clockwise from top left)* Robert W. Young/FPG International; © Paul Barton/The Stock Market; © Roy Morsch/The Stock Market; © Paul Barton/The Stock Market

# Author's Acknowledgments

A great number of people assisted in writing *Interchange Intro*. Particular thanks go to the following:

The **students** and **teachers** in the following schools and institutes who pilot tested components of *Interchange Intro*; their valuable comments and suggestions helped shape the content of the entire course:

**Adult ESL Resource Centre,** Toronto, Canada; **The Bickford Centre,** Toronto, Canada; **Centro Cultural Salvadreño,** El Salvador; **Centro Internacional de Idiomas Maestros Asociados, S.C.,** Mexico; **Connections Language Consultants, Inc.,** Edmonton, Canada; **Dorset College,** Vancouver, Canada; **English Academy,** Japan; **Eurocentres,** Alexandria, Virginia, U.S.A.; **Fairmont State University,** West Virginia, U.S.A.; **Truman College,** Chicago, Illinois, U.S.A.; **Instituto Cultural de Idiomas Ltda,** Brazil; **Instituto Mexicano-Norteamericano de Cultura,** Mexico; **Language Resources,** Kobe, Japan; **Nippon Information and Communication Co.,** Japan; **Tokushima Bunri University,** Japan; and **University of California at Los Angeles Extension**, California, U.S.A.

And **editors** and **advisors** at Cambridge University Press, who provided guidance during the complex process of writing classroom materials:

Suzette André, Colin Bethell, Sarah Coleman, Riitta da Costa, Steve Dawson, Peter Donovan, Sandra Graham, Colin Hayes, John Haywood, Steven Maginn, Jane Mairs, Carine Mitchell, Noreen O'Connor-Abel, Susan Ryan, Helen Sandiford, Chuck Sandy, Ellen Shaw, Koen Van Landeghem, and Mary Vaughn.